POWWOW COUNTRY
PEOPLE OF THE CIRCLE

BY CHRIS ROBERTS

PUBLISHED BY MEADOWLARK PUBLISHING COMPANY

Right: *Terry Fiddler, Sioux, pauses for a bite to eat at a popular food stand during the 1994 Red Bottom Celebration in Frazer, Montana. Terry is a renowned champion Northern Traditional dancer who competes and officiates at powwows from coast to coast. Even though he makes his home in South Dakota, he travels regularly to this mid-June celebration to visit his Assiniboine friends and relations on the Fort Peck Reservation. Terry's satin shirt is embroidered with felt designs in a similar manner to beaded buckskin warshirts. This manner of decorating cloth shirts, which developed in Sioux country, has become popular with Traditional dancers in the past several years.*

Front cover: *Lonny Street, Comanche/Mesquakie, Traditional dancer at North American Indian Days in Browning, Montana.*

Back cover: *A Fancy Shawl dancer observes the Grand Entry ceremonies at Rocky Boy's Memorial Powwow.*

Page 1: *Cleveland High Bull (Holy Elk Boy), Sioux, acts as a flag bearer at Lame Deer, Montana.*

ISBN: 1-56037-124-2

For additional copies of this book contact: Meadowlark Publishing Company, P.O. Box 7218, Missoula, MT 59807 or Call 1-888-728-2180

REG
Coffe
Lg .75
Sm. .50

DEDICATION

This book is dedicated to the memory of Lloyd Runsabove, Oglala Lakota, and Margaret Red Cherries Runsabove, Northern Cheyenne, who welcomed me, and initiated a family bond that continues to enrich and grow. True cultural people whose children pass on traditions to their children, they always encouraged their family to appreciate native ways.

Above: Detail of Lonny Street's chest decoration. Note how Lonny's beadwork coordinates with the rest of his regalia.

Facing page: Donny Rain, a Stoney Traditional dancer from Canada, wears striking face paint, rings, and earrings at the 1997 Rocky Boy's Memorial Powwow.

A young Jingle Dress competitor checks out her fellow dancers before a contest at Rocky Boy.

CONTENTS

FOREWORD by Bonnie Heavy Runner Craig 11

PREFACE 15

PART 1—PEOPLE OF THE CIRCLE 21

PART 2—DANCERS OF THE CIRCLE 47

PART 3—A CIRCLE OF EVENTS 67

PART 4—A CIRCLE OF LIFE 79

BIBLIOGRAPHY AND VIDEOGRAPHY 126

Keith Nehanee, a Squamish/Hawaiian Traditional dancer from British Columbia, gets low at Spokane, Washington's Riverfront Park.

FOREWORD

BY BONNIE HEAVY RUNNER CRAIG
DIRECTOR, NATIVE AMERICAN STUDIES DEPARTMENT
UNIVERSITY OF MONTANA-MISSOULA

Native people live their lives with symbols. Interpreting and seeing meaning behind each event equates to learning. In tribal groups, the shared aspect of understanding these connections begins at or before birth. The circle is the strongest symbol of connection to cultural identity and expression. If one looks carefully at western society and various ways people join in expressing it, one can see the round dance in cowboy culture. In our world, ethnic groups come together to enjoy who they are.

In Native culture, the circle is expressed through ceremony, art, spirituality, and socializing. The warm feeling of joining a round dance or owl dance can rejuvenate the oldest heart. Non-verbal communication that is allowed when you join a circle have few bounds for individuals. We were meant to know who we are and this is expressed through the circle. Ceremonies follow the sun. Each placement of a person or object has meaning and connection to the whole being. Because of the circle, the intent to be whole does not have an alternative in sacred ceremony or dance.

Today, Indian people speak of "the sacred hoop" in terms of healing cultural oppression and exploring grief. Once again the circle provides the symbol of expression. Dances that touch the circle in an arbor or hall follow the same pattern.

When you look behind the symbolism, you see children, young men and women, elders all coming together as equals in a joyous expression of who they are. The elders smile as the infant wanders onto the dance floor. "Look," says Grandma, Auntie or Uncle, "They're part of us. Make room!"

The circle expands and embraces the child. The tribe is stronger and happiness abounds. ✠

Above: *Two young teen boys wait for the next intertribal at the Nez Perce's Chief Looking Glass Powwow in Kamiah, Idaho. The young man on the left carries a full beaded dance stick and wears eagle feathers while the dancer on the right uses hawk feathers.*

Page 10: *A Southern Style Fancy dancer "going around" the arbor at Rocky Boy wears two eagle rocker feathers in his porcupine hair headdress and hackle feather arm bustles.*

Darryl Goodwill displays beautiful floral beaded hearts on the back of his Grass dance outfit.

PREFACE

"I like this book, Chris. What you've written is good and the pictures really capture the feeling of the powwow." A Traditional dancer friend, Charlie, was looking over his newly acquired copy of *Powwow Country*. I was nervously awaiting his opinion because it mattered to me more than any media review. He was a valued critic. We had known each other for twenty-five years. As a seasoned veteran of the powwow circuit, he'd tell me if I had messed up. "There is one thing you need to fix," he added.

"What's that?" I asked with earnest concern.

"Your book doesn't have a picture of me in it! It needs less words and more pictures. It needs my picture. Do another book and put me in it," he joked.

I was in the Seattle Civic Center on Easter Sunday, 1993. I had traveled west for my first powwow of the season. *Powwow Country* had been released the previous November. I was on the circuit for the first time since its release, introducing it to vendors.

Do another book? The first one had taken me ten years from conception to publication. The ink was barely dry. Charlie had quickly scanned the book flipping through pages looking for friends and relatives and made his evaluation within minutes.

I had traveled a lot that summer. My powwow season had started on the west coast in Seattle and had ended on the east coast in Hartford, Connecticut. It had been one of the wettest, most rugged seasons I had ever experienced powwowing. As I traveled and *Powwow Country* became more well-known, I kept hearing the same message. "We'd like to see another book. More pictures next time."

So, slowly, by degrees, I made up my mind to do a second book. But how would I follow the first one? What would I write about? I had been seriously photographing American Indian celebrations for ten years. I had a good supply of images to illustrate various aspects of the powwow. My files were get-

Above: *Gary Comes at Night and Tyrone Whitegrass, both Blackfeet, visit while dancing at the North American Indian Days in Browning, Montana.*

Page 14: *A Fancy dancer's neck bustle is a swirl of color and motion as he spins during a men's contest at Rocky Boy.*

ting thicker as I photographed that entire summer, yet I did not feel I had enough images to warrant another book. A second book would have to wait.

As friends would ask me, "When is the next book coming out?" I'd respond, "I want my second book to be different than the first. I need to focus on making pictures until I have enough to capture the color and feeling I experience as a participant. I also want more of you to be in it," I added honestly. In truth, I wish **all of you** could be in this book. For the past five years, I have been making pictures of friends and family, strangers and acquaintances, in hopes I can create images that speak words. Sometimes things go well and I'm able to make an image I'm proud of. Other times, things don't. That is part of photography. I do my best to make pictures that work on many levels. I work on composition, color, content, and clarity. But most importantly, I strive for images which express spirit and culture.

I've approached *People of the Circle* differently than my previous book. *Powwow Country* was created to fill a void in literature on the strong contemporary culture of American Indian people exemplified by the powwow. It was meant to explain what is a powwow, what goes on at them, and why they are important to Indian people. It was not meant to be an all-encompassing academic treatise on the entire world of powwows. It is a recording of observations and experiences I encountered in the country in which I travel. In its case, I wrote the book first and then chose images which illustrated the text.

In *People of the Circle*, I made the pictures first, chose the better ones, and wrote to illustrate and explain those images. It is good if readers learn more about the many diverse elements that come together at powwows. But most of all, I wish the images in this book to fulfill their primary purpose: to impart the warmth and joy that exists in this world; to better understand that these native people know who they are and are happy in that knowledge; to know that if you are drawn to this circle you are welcome; to see and feel the relationship that exists between everyone present; to understand that the Creator wishes us to appreciate life and each other. It is my hope that in understanding the essence of this book you will better appreciate American Indian culture and the people of this circle. ☖

Freddy and Rob Hunter and Amy Carson and Joe Whitehawk enjoy an Owl Dance where women ask men to be dance partners at the 1995 Bitterroot Good Nations Powwow in Hamilton, Montana.

Children are children everywhere as this spirited group attests at the 1993 Schemitzun in Hartford, Connecticut. It is interesting to note the ethnic makeup of these young boys as they ham it up for the camera during an intertribal dance.

A Southern Straight dancer shows good form at Rocky Boy, Montana.

PART I

PEOPLE OF THE CIRCLE

American Indian culture is diverse and adaptive. Many of this continent's native peoples have survived and weathered the storms of acculturation which have assaulted them throughout this continent's recent history.

Today Indian culture is on a resurgence. Increasingly, native languages are taught in the classroom. Elders are appreciated for their knowledge and wisdom. Native craftspeople, artisans, and entertainers are gaining national recognition for their talent and skill. American Indian music is growing in scope and popularity. Tribal business leaders are achieving increased success in managing their own resources. Traditional tribal gambling, sometimes referred to as the new buffalo, has evolved into income-generating casinos for many impoverished reservations. Medical practitioners are looking at native curing techniques to augment their abilities in providing health care both on and off tribal lands.

Today, social celebrations of Indian life commonly referred to as powwows are proliferating at a rapid rate throughout the North American continent. Many tribes are adopting this plains cultural event as a way of strengthening or stimulating interest in their heritage. Powwows can be seen as the large and visible point of a cultural pyramid with awareness and interest of other native ways related to their popularity and proliferation. As this powwow world has grown over the past quarter century, so has it evolved and adapted in our ever-changing world.

The powwow has been introduced to parts of the continent in which it never existed twenty-five years ago. Today powwows are being adopted by tribes that never had them as part of their history. The Seminoles of Florida, the Navajos and Pueblos of the Southwest, even coastal Indians on both sides of the continent host powwows. Powwows have joined the feathered warbonnet and tipi as a way of saying "this is Indian." Indian culture has been experiencing this widespread rejuvenation and growth since the mid-1970s. Powwows are at the forefront of this "cultural renaissance."

On a magnificent midsummer day without a cloud in the brilliant, blue sky, a loud shot punctuated the morning quiet. The cannon's sharp report foretold that the parade was proceeding down the dusty, windblown streets of Browning, Montana. Glowing wintry white, the distant snow-capped Rocky Mountains of Glacier National Park provided an intense backdrop for the parade wending its way down Main Street.

North American Indian Days, a celebration of the Blackfeet nation, is one of the major Northern Plains powwows on the summer circuit. Several thousand people swell the streets of this northwest-central Montana town to one of the main events of this highly respected annual powwow.

A powwow is not limited to dancing and singing "Indian" but is the term given to a celebration of culture. The powwow is like a giant family reunion whose attendance can double a reservation's population. Tribes or organizations host powwows for their own pleasure, and while held year-round, traffic on the powwow trail drastically increases between Memorial Day and Labor Day.

The word *powwow* is from the Algonquian Tribe's language for a meeting of medicine men or spiritual leaders. It was called a "pau wau." The white settlers

Above: *John Grounds, Blackfeet, watches the arbor action while taking a break before his Traditional dance contest. John incorporates items friends have given him with things that pertain to his life into his dance clothes. He is able to tell a story about everything he wears.*

Page 20: *1996 World Champion Northern Traditional dancer Tom Christian, Sioux, shows off his young son Thomas Jr. on Father's Day at the Red Bottom Celebration. When Tom isn't dancing he shares his cultural knowledge working with the Poplar Montana Public School District.*

Right: Keith Nehanee, Squamish / Hawaiian, displays an eagle feather visor and a quilled wheel hair decoration and a unique beaded neck choker from which hang deer dew claws.

Below: Women's Jingle Dress dancers line up to have their competition numbers noted for the afternoon Grand Entry at Browning, Montana.

in the colonial times construed the word to mean any gathering of Indian people.

In the later 1800s and early 1900s, both the United States and Canadian governments attempted to repress Native culture and traditions.

Celebrations of Indian culture were frowned upon. It wasn't until the civil rights movements of the 1950s and 1960s that expressions of culture were hailed as a way of building a future.

Renewed interest in powwows by Indians and non-Indians alike has created a dramatic increase in the number of these events in the United States and Canada. Powwows can be found in every state of the union including Hawaii. A recent calendar lists over 1,200 in North America. Entire families travel to the big powwows, often setting up their tents and tipis in the same spot as the previous year.

Powwows range in size from small tribal powwows to large intertribal events that attract thousands. Tribal powwows bring people together from a single reservation or community to dance and visit in a social and festive atmosphere.

Intertribal powwows are major events and massive undertakings. These events require heavy fund raising to provide for expenses and dancers' contest prize money. Admission to outdoor reservation powwows is rarely charged.

Drum groups and dancers from all over the United States and Canada travel days to attend a favorite intertribal powwow. At big events like Gathering of Nations in Albuquerque, New Mexico, (April) or United Tribes in Bismarck, North Dakota, (September) over 100 tribes can easily be represented. Montana's Crow Fair (August) attracts attendees from as far away as Germany and England.

The powwow has its own professional participants akin to rodeo or car racing. Many dancers and

Above: Fancy dancers and long-time friends, Corey Roberts and Walter Runsabove, smile for the camera at Rocky Boy, Montana. Walter's Indian name, "His Horse That Flys," is embroidered on his vest. Corey was given the name "Whirlwind" by Walter's father, Bill Runsabove.

Facing page: Bob Boyer Jr., a Red River Metis born in Prince Albert, Saskatchewan, dances in an Old Style Northern Traditional outfit at the Bitterroot Good Nations Powwow. This style is currently gaining in popularity and some powwows are now setting up both Old Style Traditional and Contemporary Traditional categories in their dance contests. Note Bob's mirrored otter breastplate, "granny" sunglasses, and lazy stitched armbands, cuffs, and kneebands. Bob is a school teacher on the Flathead Reservation in Charlo, Montana.

singers earn their livelihood during a season on the circuit. Others make their living by operating food or craft concessions, and still others receive fees as announcers or arena directors.

As these events spread into various regions of the continent the inhabitants of these cultural regions add their influence to the powwow world. The gambling-rich Mashantucket Pequots of Connecticut host Schemitzun (September), the world's richest powwow, with one million dollars in prize monies. Now other regions of the country struggle to raise high prize monies and payouts in order to attract top name dancers and singers.

These cultural differences affect dance regalia. Narragansets from the East Coast incorporate sea shells and traditional tribal attire into their powwow clothes. Navajo powwow dancers have to decide whether to adopt a Northern Plains or a Southern Plains look, sometimes blending both. Seminoles have influenced powwow clothes. Now some "ribbon shirts" sport Seminole-style patchwork cloth designs. Sioux beadwork designs are being incorporated into cloth shirts for Northern Traditional dancers.

Over the past twenty years, fringe on northern Grass dance outfits has changed from chainette shawl fringe to white strung yarn, then to colored strung yarn. Today satin ribbons are becoming a popular new look. Some Grass dancers have intricately sewn shoulder capes, pants and aprons as the main feature of their outfits. This allows dancers to adopt a freer, more active style of movement because they no longer wear heavy beaded harnesses and belts.

Dance clothes are becoming increasingly more ornate. In areas of the country where powwowing is relatively new, dancers will choose to adopt one of the basic styles that has existed for the past fifty years. As they become comfortable and familiar with dancing, dancers look to their own tribal heritage for influences to incorporate into their regalia. A

Above: A Traditional dancer's beaded vest uses a Northern Plains Sioux tipi design with a more contemporary background. This teen dancer's entire outfit all matched.

Facing page: Delbert Wapass from the Thunder Child Reserve in Saskatchewan demonstrates his winning Grass dance form. Like many powwow people, Delbert passes his cultural knowledge on to young people as an educator and teacher.

Jingle Dress action in the Hartford, Connecticut, Civic Arena at Schemitzun '93, the World Championship of Singing and Dance. Even though this powwow, sponsored by the wealthy Mashantucket/Pequot Tribe, is relatively new on the national circuit, it is well known for the large amount of prize money it offers. Proceeds from gambling revenue at the tribe's Foxwoods Casino helped establish this event, thus influencing other reservations and communities to sponsor "casino powwows."

Nez Perce will wear a cornhusk bag, while the Lakota's bag will be lazy-stitch beaded. Tribal designs show up in beadwork. An experienced observer can tell where a dancer originates by the subtle yet distinct differences in the basic elements of dance clothes.

As outfits evolve, dance categories also evolve. Some powwows are differentiating "new" looks from old ones by developing sub-categories within categories of dance contests. At major powwows there is now Old Style Grass Dance and Contemporary Grass Dance. A dancer chooses whether to be an Old Style Traditional or a more modern, and usually quite elaborate, Contemporary Traditional dancer.

Some older style dances are gaining in popularity. For example, an early style of Fancy Dance in the Northern Plains is now re-emerging as a traditional style referred to as Chicken Dance. Jingle dress dancers, popular in the 1920s, all but vanished in the 1960s. Jingle Dress is now one of the most popular women's dance styles.

As new materials become available and emphasis on fine dance clothes increases, outfits are becoming ever more elaborate and costly. What was a "killer" outfit twenty years ago is now relatively average. Northern Traditional women's beaded dress tops are becoming extremely ornate. Some outfits feature natural scenes, animals, geometric or floral designs entirely beaded in the more expensive cut beads. Dancers have several changes of outfits so they can catch a judge's eye in the daytime and then switch to a "nighttime outfit" that stands out more vibrantly under the lights of the arbor for an evening session.

Professional dance companies of powwow dancers are springing up around the continent, spurred on by the success of the American Indian Dance Theater. The Dance Theater broke new ground by producing two Public Broadcasting System television programs featuring dancers presenting powwow dance

Merle Eaglespeaker, Blood/Yakama, in striking face paint, has just won the Long Knife family's men's Traditional contest at the 1997 Milk River Indian Days in Fort Belknap, Montana. Merle wears beautiful thematic appliqué beadwork combining his epaulets with eagle feather "shoulder wings."

Yellow and black colors used throughout a men's Traditional dancer's clothes are sometimes referred to as "bumblebee outfits." This dancer carries the concept into his shield design with one slight deviation.

systems. Now big name singing groups have top-of-the-line equipment with mixing boards and powerful speakers. Indoor powwows incorporate an arena's sound system to amplify the singers and assistants carry wireless microphones from drum group to drum group. One singer predicts, "It's possible, as wireless clip-on mikes become more accessible, each member of a group will have his own microphone."

Technological advances not only assist dancers and singers but are also manifested in dance arenas. Powwows in urban areas like Hartford, Seattle, or Albuquerque take place in large civic facilities. In Winnipeg, Ontario, dancers' award ceremonies benefitted from special effects like mirror balls, spotlights, and fog machines. Grace Gillette of the Denver March Powwow has developed a software program allowing judges to tabulate a dancer's points on computer so by the powwows' completion the computer determines the winner and prints out pay envelopes.

styles and a Northwest coast tribe's "giving" of a regional/tribal dance to members of the troupe to perform.

This company sends out talent scouts on the circuit to recruit top dancers, assembles them in New York City, and then incorporates their powwow dancing into a cohesive show. The company is able to book shows in Europe and the Orient for over $10,000 per performance. Following this example, the Mashantucket Pequots have formed the Foxwoods Dance Troupe, while another company sponsored by the Seminole tribe performed at the 1996 Olympics in Atlanta.

Powwow campgrounds can be rugged places to camp. Hot sun, lack of shade, dust, and insects all make living outdoors difficult. However many participants' lives are more comfortable and relaxed as

Plateau Women's Traditional dress back incorporating pony beads, rocaille beads and cowrie shells with a panel belt.

Indian people have always been quick to adopt what is new and better to improve their lives. The horse replaced the dog, canvas replaced buffalo hide tipis, and beads replaced porcupine quills. Twenty-five years ago few drum groups had public address

Popular video arcade games entertain the young with their own particular slant in powwow concession stand trailers.

entire families travel in self-contained recreational vehicles.

Even though it is miles from the nearest large town, and situated on a windswept, treeless bluff, Rocky Boy's Memorial Powwow (August) dance floor was leveled and sodded for the 1996 event by a professional landscape company. Oregon's Siletz tribe has developed their powwow grounds so well that campers are provided with a laundry, hot showers, lots of shade, and picnic tables in a pristine woodland park. In Lincoln City, only thirty miles from the powwow grounds, the tribe's Chinook Winds Casino provides top name entertainment in a newly opened, tastefully designed, multi-million-dollar facility.

Change also comes to powwow concessions. Many stands still sell the old standbys of pop, coffee, and freshly squeezed lemonade, but others are opting for espresso, lattes, and cappucinos. A hungry camper can buy fry bread, burgers, or Indian tacos, as well as flame-broiled shish kabobs, Greek gyros or Thai spring rolls. Up in Canada a Toronto vendor is heading cross country on the circuit selling East Indian curried pizza.

Non-food concessions offer everything from dance supplies and handmade beadwork to computerized sewing of fancy satin jackets or ball caps. Kids can amuse themselves buying toys, jumping on trampolines, or playing in a mobile video arcade.

Other, more deep-seated changes have taken place in the past twenty-five years. The powwow world has been affected by the women's movement. In the 1960s most women sang standing behind male singers sitting at the drum; now women not only

sing sitting at the drum, but serve as lead singers.

The continuing emergence of women affects many aspects of Indian society. Women are willing to speak out more. Women serve on powwow committees. As this trend continues there is an increasing possibility that long-time traditional male powwow roles such as arena director, announcer, and flag bearers will be handled by women, as well.

With its acceptance of intertribal values and cultural diversity, the powwow world today is quicker to adapt and accept changes. As these changes occur in the dance circle they will carry over into the circle of everyday life.

"Powwow people recognize themselves. Being a powwow person is a feeling, a way of being and acting. People on the circuit care about each other. They learn to treat others with respect because they know they fall into one of two categories. You're either a host or a visitor," Merle Tendoy, a well-known Chippewa-Cree announcer, told me. "If you are a visitor, you learn generosity because you are treated well by your hosts. When it is your turn to be a host, you must treat your visitors good or they won't come to your celebration. When you host a powwow its best to have a good heart to ensure it having a good spirit," Merle concluded.

Traveling is part of powwow life. Art Scalplock, a Blood whose family is grown, travels the circuit from spring to fall. "I always wanted to be able to do this, to travel from powwow to powwow without caring where I was going next or having to go home to work. Now I basically live out of my car, though I maintain a mailing address in Seattle," he told me at the 99th Annual Arlee Powwow. "Maybe one weekend you make nine hundred dollars and you use half the money to repair your car, the rest goes towards living expenses, and a few bills back home. The next weekend I may do even better so I put aside cash for Christmas, give some to family members, and save some for those weekends when I don't hit in the money or am a bit short."

People who travel continually from celebration to celebration depend on their hosts for a good ex-

Above: *Due to the late night events, participants have to catch sleep when and where they can. In this case it's in a cozy car on the Lame Deer powwow grounds.*

Facing page: *Grass dancers shaking hands with each other after a contest session in Browning, Montana.*

Tribal Chairman John Sun Child, carrying the Indian flag, welcomes visitors during the Grand Entry ceremonies at Rocky Boy's 1995 Memorial Powwow.

perience and the necessities of life. They need shelter, a place to pitch a tent or a roof over their heads. Water and sanitation facilities are essential. These basic items can make or break an event.

But the host's responsibilities don't stop with the basics. Hospitality is the key issue. A powwow may be sponsored by a tribe or an organization, but all members of the community pitch in to make visitors feel good. Next-door neighbors will offer morning coffee, local residents invite campers to "come clean up." Announcements like, "The showers are open at the tribal Recreation Hall," or, "Visitors are asked to come over to the south side of camp. The Long Knife family is sponsoring a feed in honor of their daughter," are truly appreciated and welcome after a long night of dancing, singing and socializing.

Food is an essential of life and hosts usually attempt to provide as much as they can. Children and adults jump from pickup trucks handing out sacks of groceries as "rations are distributed" to the entire camp. Anyone with a tent, tipi, trailer or recreation vehicle on the grounds is considered a guest of the powwow committee and their stay is made easier by the gift of food.

"Treat your visitors good and they will tell their friends. Your powwow will grow and become popular. People will enjoy themselves. Create good feelings and a good feeling will be your reward." Powwow people understand this unwritten rule. "Welcome everyone. Your visitors have traveled far to be with you," an elder counseled the United Peoples committee as they made plans for a new powwow on the circuit.

"You want all present to have good times helping them to forget bad ones. The circle is a place of healing, a place to get well," the wise man said. "Powwows are celebrations. There is no room for bad thoughts or feelings at a celebration."

Besides hosts and visitors, people can be classified into two other categories. These are participants and spectators. Both are an integral part of a successful celebration. Dancers, singers, officials, honorees, concessionaires, security, and committee members are all participants. However, at other times they may be spectators. "It's relaxing to sit in the cool shade of an arbor all afternoon and watch the world go by around you." Whether it's a dance contest, an intertribal, an exhibition, or giveaway, things happen. Powwow people tend to be people-watchers and content themselves to sit and observe activities for long periods of time without any concern for clocks or schedules.

Walking around the arbor is another pastime which allows for people-watching. Kids cavort, laughing and giggling, chasing each other. Teens chase each other too, but with different intent, sometimes asking friends to arrange introductions with the opposite sex. Spectators have time to chat, moving from friend to friend like bees from flower to flower, perhaps stopping to peruse a craft stand or sip hot coffee on a cool night. Being a spectator makes it easier to engage in powwow socialization.

Dancers visit before the evening dance session at Frazer, Montana. Baseball caps comfortably replace headdresses while waiting for events to begin.

Whereas a spectator's range of activity is simple and relaxing, a participant's can be hurried, hectic, and harried depending on their degree of involvement. The most visible and hard working participants are the dancers, singers, officials and head people who organize and officiate over powwow events.

While dancers are the most colorful and visible participants of a powwow, it is the singers who are the most important. A group of singers, commonly referred to as a drum group, provides the music for the dancers. Small powwows may have as little as one or two drum groups whereas large northern powwows like Crow Fair or United Tribes in Bismarck, North Dakota, may have as many as thirty. Good music is a key element to the success of a powwow.

"If you have good singers, the dancers will come, no matter the amount of prize money. It's the song that makes dancers want to get out there and move. The drum provides the beat. Good drum groups get the dancers onto the dance floor. Good songs get them to dance well," says Bill Runsabove, a singer for the Badlands Singers.

Popular drum groups always attract "recorders" around them. The Black Lodge Singers from White Swan, Washington, draw their usual crowd at the University of Montana's Kyi Yo Powwow in Missoula.

Arena Director Chico Her Many Horses, a Sioux from South Dakota, lines up tiny tots for a Grand Entry at Fort Belknap. Chico established his reputation as a trend-setting Fancy dancer in the 1970s. Today he still dances but also officiates at many powwows.

To the unfamiliar listener, Indian singing sounds exotic and difficult to comprehend. To the experienced ear, melodies flow, ascend and descend.

Songs with vocables (vowel sounds of ya, hey, hi, lay, loi, etc.) have no meaning but carry the tune of the song. They correspond to tones and notes. A lead singer begins with the first line of a song's chorus which is then followed by a "second singer" who repeats the line with variations in pitch and tone. Then the rest of the group joins in singing. Accentuated drum beats indicate the break between the chorus and the verse. Repeating a chorus and verse four times constitutes a full song. The speed and volume of the last five beats of the song indicates its end, allowing the dancers to stop on the last beat.

As powwows evolve and become more complex, more people are needed to help them run smoothly. The arena director is one of the most important positions at a powwow.

Many times arena directors are chosen because of their abilities as dancers and their knowledge of dance contests. Jonathan Windy Boy, a renowned grass dancer, serves frequently as arena director at his home celebration in Rocky Boy. He controls activities on the dance floor. Arena directors choose judges, distribute and collect contest ballots, schedule giveaways and specials, and assist with arranging the dance contests over the course of the day. His duties leave Windy Boy with little time for sleep. He is one of the first people to get things going in the morning and one of the last to leave late at night. Jonathan stays in shape for dancing by literally run-

Southern Straight dancers observe the opening ceremonies after the Grand Entry at Rocky Boy.

ning around the arbor all day long as he sees to the continual progression of arena events.

◻

In close harmony and contact with the arena director are announcers who also assist in making schedules run as smoothly as possible. Announcers keep the audience informed as to activities which will take place in the arena, announcing contests, specials, activities, calling out for lost children, parents, or spouses, telling jokes, and explaining the various activities taking place. Popular announcers are paid for their organizational and speaking skills and many receive travel expenses to preside over powwows far from home.

◻

Dance contest judges are selected because of their knowledge, experience, and exposure to good dancing. Sometimes judges are simply selected by the arena

director who hands out ballots before a contest. Other times judges may be selected by family members sponsoring a dance contest. These judges may be relations and friends of the family or may be selected because of their dancing or singing skills. Judges take their role seriously and do the best they can in a difficult task. To avoid favoritism judges usually quietly refrain from judging a particular contest if a relative is competing.

Dancers are judged on style according to age groups within their particular category. Dancing off-beat, dropping a part of regalia, or failing to stop on the last beat of the drum reduces a contestant's points.

Noted dancers, distinguished tribal members, and veterans participate in arena events as flag bearers. These people are given the honor of carrying national, state, provincial, tribal, or military veterans' flags in the Grand Entry of dancers which begins each session. It is a great honor to be selected to carry the Indian flag, a decorated coup stick, which represents Indian people everywhere. Elders, tribal officials, powwow committee leaders, local or visiting princesses and other selected honorees may participate by giving an opening welcome or leading a blessing of "all those gathered here to celebrate being together again."

Non-arena participants include the many concessionaires who provide goods, souvenirs, and essentials like food and drink to both the hosts and visitors at powwows. They spend long days catering to a variety of needs of powwow people and guests who come to watch the weekend events. Many

A Vietnam veteran carries the Indian flag in Hartford, Connecticut.

The Northern Cheyenne Veterans Color Guard "present colors" at the Big Sky Powwow in Helena, Montana.

concessionaires are seen year after year at the same powwows, set up in the same spot they had in previous years. Concession fees help support the powwow and pay expenses.

Powwows are also judged by the quality and number of concessionaires. A key relationship exists between the concessionaires, the visitors and the spectators. The concessionaires need lots of attending people to "make their fee." Attending people need a broad variety of concessions to draw many of them to the event. As long as people are present, concessions stay open, providing both goods and a bustling market atmosphere. For many people there is great enjoyment in "cruising the stands in the cool of night," searching for the best fry bread, good stew, tripe, the right key chain, the newest powwow cassette tape, or the right craft supplies for a particular project.

Again, friends are made and bonds reaffirmed at concession stand stops. A powwow with few concessions can be a pretty dull place before or after the arena activities take place.

Gambling is a big part of many powwows. Stick game songs can be heard day and night drawing both locals and visitors into days-long tournaments. Others try their luck at cards, keno and bingo, or various kinds of electronic machines taking and giving out money beneath large pavilion tents or gambling arbors.

Terry Brockie, Gros Ventre, encourages a young dancer to "get out there" at North American Indian Days.

Patrolling the grounds, taking care of injuries or incidents, seeing to it that the peace is kept are "the security." Both uniformed police and T-shirted security can be seen carrying long four-celled flashlights as a tool of the trade. Patrol cars cruise the outer perimeters of camps while those on foot walk around the area insuring that problems will be taken care of with efficiency. Twenty-five to thirty years ago, problems were caused by alcohol consumption. In the intervening years, there has been an intense emphasis on powwows being alcohol- and substance-

Police agencies cooperate to provide security in powwow camp communities. Just like any cop walking a beat, they gather for coffee and a donut at the "Powwow Kitchen."

free. Peer pressure and a firm commitment by everyone involved has eliminated abuse and created a family environment. Miscreants and violators are met with comments and clear messages of "Take it some place else. You are not wanted here if you can't abide by the rules. This is not the place for alcohol nor rowdy behavior." Powwows reaffirm the fact that you don't have to abuse drugs or alcohol to have a good time. Theft and vandalism in powwow camps is almost unheard of. Belongings are safely left on camp tables or arbor chairs with little concern. Cops are occasionally asked to break up a fight, but most of the time their duties deal with lost children, minor first aid or clearing blocked vehicles. Their presence insures the peace and provides a blanket of security throughout the celebration. Their vigilance continues to reinforce the powwow's reputation as being a safe and happy place for the entire family.

The powwow brings people together in a common purpose. Family members reconnect with each other and other families. Hands of friendship extend to other tribes and cultures. A network of support strengthens an entire race of people.

Tribal members reaffirm their heritage and identity. To be Indian is to be proud, to know who you are, where you came from. Knowing these things helps Indian people guide their future, while the interaction of children and elders ensures a continuation of culture. The powwow provides the center in which all of this takes place. It is the circle of life. ✠

Right: Todd George, Yakama, and Terry Fiddler get dressed at their campsite in Frazer, Montana.

Below: John Windy Boy, Chippewa/Cree, shares a popular powwow circuit soda and a laugh. A champion dancer from a very young age, John and his mother Darlene were tragically killed in an automobile accident in 1995. John will always be remembered as an exuberant personality who had the ability to make those around him laugh and feel good. He made friends easily and is deeply missed by all those he touched in his too-short life.

Three different Northern Plains women's dance styles are apparent side by side as these three ladies circle the dance floor at Fort Belknap. The arbor floor is most crowded when dancers enjoy the first set of intertribals immediately following a Grand Entry. Left to right, the styles are Jingle Dress, Traditional, and Patty Young Running Crane in Fancy Shawl.

PART 2

DANCERS OF THE CIRCLE

"When you 'dance Indian' you must dance with every part of your body, not just your feet," Bill Runsabove instructed me many years ago when I was a beginning dancer. Back in the early 1970s, Bill, a Sioux/Cheyenne from Lame Deer, Montana, was a champion Fancy dancer. Today he is an honored member of the Badlands Singers on the Fort Peck Reservation and travels all over the continent singing and officiating at powwows. Bill's fifteen-year-old son Walter follows in his dad's moccasin tracks as a winning fancy dancer with Bill coaching him and offering advice.

"Back when I started dancing Northern Fancy we only danced with a single back bustle. This was before the influence of the Southern Fancy dancers and their back and neck bustles. You had to dance with good footwork and use more movement. You had to use more of your body, especially your head and shoulders," Bill told me recently.

Bill continued, "My dad, Lloyd Runsabove, an Oglalla Sioux, told me that judges look at a dancer's head movements as much as their footwork. 'You have to move your whole body and make your headress feathers spin constantly to catch the judges' attention,' Dad said. Dad also taught me the two eagle feathers in a dancers porcupine hair headress were called 'enemy feathers' for brave deeds against an enemy," Bill added.

On the modern-day powwow circuit, styles of "outfits" or "regalia" correspond to dance styles, whether Fancy dance, Traditional dance, Men's Grass dance, or Women's Jingle Dress dance.

"Costumes are worn by clowns or actors. We wear outfits. We are taught to respect these dance clothes as they are special to us and our families," Addie Many Chief, a Blood elder told me.

Men's and women's Fancy dancers are typified

Above: A Traditional dancer, Wilbert Beebe, at Spokane, Washington's Riverfront Park.

Page 46: Southern Fancy dancer Mike Roberts, Choctaw / Chickasaw, "hits a good song" during an intertribal at Rocky Boy's.

by brilliant, flashy colors accompanied with a highly energetic, exuberant, fast dance style with lots of spinning and intricate footwork. The men wear bright feather neck and back bustles and the women drape an embroidered shawl around their shoulders using it "like the wings of a butterfly."

Most male dancers wear a porcupine and dyed deer hair headdress sometimes referred to as a "porky roach." This is tied on with a "spreader." This device spreads the hair out like the crest of a male bird during courting. The dancer's head is further decorated with a matching beaded headband to which "scalp feathers" are often attached. Male and female

dancers will often wear earrings. Necks will be covered with bone bead "chokers" or scarves.

Grass dancers do not wear bustles but wear a pants and shirt combination which is decorated with brightly colored yarn or ribbon fringes. Grass dancers wear similar head decoration as fancy dancers and wear either two eagle "spinner" feathers or eagle plumes attached to springs or stripped quills in the spreader. Grass dancers dance with a loose-limbed, relaxed, yet strenuous style with lots of body and foot movement.

A young admirer and future dancer shakes hands as participants and spectators alike partake in a Round dance at North American Indian Days. Round dances are social dances where everyone present is invited to join in regardless of being in regalia or not. As the circle expands to accommodate participants, rings of dancers will face each other. One ring dances clockwise, the other counter clockwise, allowing people to exchange a smile and a handshake.

Male and female Traditional dancers wear natural outfits. Men wear hawk and eagle feather bustles and bone breastplates. Buckskin capes, leggings, and aprons are decorated with fringe and older beadwork patterns and colors. In addition to porcupine hair roaches, traditional dancers can wear feathered bonnets and visors or animal hide headdresses. Dancers thrust out their chests, bend low and carefully move their head and body with deliberate actions. They re-enact warriors searching for an enemy or hunters stalking prey.

Most female powwow dancers usually wear either a single eagle feather or plume in their hair. Women's head decorations can be influenced by cultural regions. For example women from the Northwest Plateau wear woven or beaded conical hats, and dancers from the Southern Plains wear a beaded headband "crown." Jingle dress dancers will sometimes intricately braid their hair or let it flow loose.

Male powwow dancers use face paint as an integral part of their head decoration. Though face painting probably originated with the "war paint" of historical times, dancers draw from family, tribal, or pan-Indian cultural influences. Recently, dancers have been drawing from cultures other than their own. Indian people have always been adaptive, taking what attracts them and incorporating it into their own cultures.

Dancers primarily use greasepaint to apply designs, initially using fingers then refining it with a brush. Fancy dancers will wear bright colors, though most dancers stick with combinations of red, yellow, blue, black or white. As in all things, powwow face painting is affected by trends. Some years everyone is in bright

Traditional dancers Art Scalplock, Blood, and Merle Carlson, Blackfeet, need sunglasses for the bright northern Montana sun in Browning.

Kevin Haywahe, a Canadian Assiniboine Traditional dancer, wears a wolf headdress which signifies his Indian name, Powerful Walking Wolf. Encouraged by his grandfather to start dancing as a child, Kevin has placed in over four hundred dance contests since he began competing.

complex face paint, and in other years, the face may be left unadorned or accentuated with a simple stripe.

There is nothing more striking than seeing a Fancy dancer whirling and twirling or a Traditional dancer executing a "fancy stop" or "move," wearing eye-catching head decorations accentuated by face paint. Dance judges look for competitors who stand out, and dancers' head decorations sometimes gives them the edge they need to win powwow dance contests.

Just as the powwow is evolving, adapting, and able to change with the times, so are dancing regalia and styles. New materials, craft items, and tribal influences allow dancers to design and incorporate these elements into their outfits. Fashions and fads peak and ebb. Change creates changes, and just as things change, so do they stay the same. Certain key parts of outfits are constant. Fancy dancers tend to be bright and flashy. Traditional dancers are more subdued. Grass dancers continue to define their outfits with flowing fringe while experimenting with makeup and layout. Currently, ribbons are popular as a trendy and colorful material for fringe. Today, more dancers are looking back to older styles of grass dancing for inspiration. Chainette shawl fringe is making a comeback in Traditional Grass dance.

Northern Traditional women's beaded dress tops are becoming larger and heavier. Jingle Dress dancers are developing more complex patterns in the placement of tin cone jingles. Some dancers favor large heavy cones, while others use smaller cones with a lighter sound. Bright cottons and satins are being supplemented with brocades and sequins. Many outfits literally sparkle under the lights at night.

Fancy Shawl dancers are designing shawls with thematic patterns and experimenting with fringe materials. For example, Hanna House, Oneida, of Wisconsin, received the concept of her monarch butterfly wing shawl in a vision.

Above: R.G. Harris, Southern Style Fancy dancer in action.
Facing page: Jingle Dress action at Kamiah, Idaho.

Primarily, the photographs in this section speak for themselves, allowing the reader to see similarities and differences within dance categories. The observations noted are meant more to point out unique variations within the dance categories rather than being the last word on the style itself. Each dancer incorporates his/her tribal background and personality into outfits that reflect who they are without always intentionally doing so. Elements of a dancer's regalia may be items that a friend has given them, other items may be made by family members or constructed by dancers themselves. Dance outfits are individual, tribal, regional, and are affected by a variety of influences. If a dancer primarily travels to local powwows, one usually sees regional tribal char-

Teen Grass dancers, Arlen Sharp and Merle Kicking Woman, Blackfeet, are making last-minute adjustments before their contest. Dancers lose their concentration if parts of their outfits are too loose or tight. Dancers can be disqualified from a contest session if a part of their regalia drops to the dance floor.

acteristics within the dance clothes. If dancers travel over a broader area, their outfits may be influenced by a current fad on the circuit or decorative variations may originate from a cultural region other than a dancer's own.

Several years ago, many male Traditional dancers were wearing loose, feathered headdresses, sometimes referred to as Mandan bonnets. Currently, it appears the porcupine hair roach is regaining its position as the most prominent headdress.

Today, many male Traditional dancers are wearing feathered "wings" as shoulder decorations. Some dancers are wearing a variation of these real feather wings by wearing a beaded cape that simulates the feathers. Another variation of these beaded, feather "wings" are beaded epaulets which do not resemble feathers at all.

Generally speaking, regalia in all dance categories is becoming more elaborate and ornate. Both genders are wearing an increasing amount of intricately designed beadwork or embroidery. Male and female Fancy dancers wear full beaded capes and in the case of men, matching aprons, kneebands, and cuffs. Other Fancy or Traditional dancers are decreasing the weight and cost of beadwork by wearing cloth outfits decorated with elaborate designs created from sequin embroidery, ribbons, or expensive fabrics. Both categories are displaying finely executed featherwork in bustles and fans.

Quillwork is making a strong comeback in the Northern Plains as crafts people are relearning and experimenting with this age-old method of decoration. Quilled wheels are fairly common while other items such as quilled armbands, kneebands, hairdrops, and breast plates are being seen in increasing numbers.

In this book, I am able to illustrate two dance styles that I was only able to talk about in my first

In this series of photos, Nathan Yabenay, Navajo, exemplifies the beauty and complexity of a Fancy dance outfit at Arlee, Montana.

Variations and similarities in Southern Straight dance clothes can be seen in this line-up of dancers in the Seattle Civic Arena during the Il-Wa-Sil powwow.

book. These are the Traditional Crow men's style and Southern Straight.

Southern Straight dance is a traditional style of regalia and dancing originating in the Southern Plains, and dancers from many tribes in that cultural region participate in it. Like all forms of "war dancing," its roots can be found in the old warrior societies. Southern Straight dancing corresponds to Northern Traditional dance. Dancers wear cloth or leather leggings "backwards" so that the decorative ribbonwork faces front. From the waist hangs front and rear aprons and a cloth trailer with matching ribbonwork. Bright satin ribbon shirts cover upper torsos. Beaded belts, woven sashes, and German silver armbands add adornment over the shirt. All Straight dancers wear an "otter drop" that extends from the back of their neck to the floor. Dancers use folded handkerchief headbands, porcupine headdresses with one eagle feather in the spreader, or otter fur turbans.

The dancers weave and glide in a stately manner around the dance floor. A sideways back and forth nodding of the head replaces the rocking motions of Fancy dance. Dancers carry "tail sticks" and mirror boards, crouching low and pointing to the drum during honor beats.

Similiar to the Southern Plains Straight dance in evolution is the modern Traditional Crow outfit. Extremely distinctive, they are always recognizable, and can't be mistaken for other tribes. "Crows are Crows," says Walter Eugene Old Elk, Sr., a champion Crow dancer. "We are a people who pride our-

Paris Leighton, Nez Perce, performs the Sneak-up in a dance contest at Rocky Boy. He "scouts for the enemy" wearing beaded scalp feathers while carrying an eagle claw dance stick, fan, and painted rawhide shield. The feathers in his bustle have been extended to create the large style of a Contemporary Northern Traditional dancer.

selves in the differences our culture has from other Plains tribes. The Crow people speak a different language, trace our heritage through our mothers, and band together in clans. Our dancing is unique and we are known for it."

The modern Crow style had its beginning in the 1920s and '30s. Crows wear brocade capes and aprons over colored tights or bare skin. Long breastplates replace traditional loop necklaces. Matching appliqued beadwork sets designed in floral or geo-metric patterns consist of a wide belt and pouch similar to a woman's, sidedrops, cuffs, armbands, and mirror bag. Contemporary bustles resemble colorful feather dusters with trailers or have eagle and hawk feathers in natural tones. Around their ankles cluster large dance bells worn over athletic socks. Crow outfits are incomplete without a string of side bells. Their porcupine headdresses are worn flat. Rooster feathers tuck into rhinestone or beaded headbands from which hang braids and long beaded drops. Dancers intricately paint their faces and sometimes rouge their lips and blush their cheeks. "The Crows are a proud people." Crow Men's Traditional is particular to the Crow Tribe, and few Crow dancers are observed outside of Montana.

Crow Traditional dancer Kenny Shane dances both Northern Traditional and the Crow way as here in a Rocky Boy Crow Belt special.

"Champion dancer." These two words are used often to describe 31 year old Traditional dancer Kevin Haywahe, an Assiniboine from Sintaluta, Saskatchewan. Kevin is one of the top Canadian dancers on the North American powwow circuit. Kevin started dancing when he was four years old, first as a Grass dancer, then switching to Traditional when he was eleven. By his estimate, Kevin has placed first in over 350 dance contests.

"My grandfather, Albert Eashappie, passed dancing on to me. He gave me my first outfit, blessed me, and gave me an eagle feather. He said that I would be the member of my family to carry our name on the powwow trail. Now all these years later I am the last of my childhood friends who is still dancing."

Kevin says that "dancing is a big part of my life. It is my way of expressing my native culture and who I am. It makes me and others feel good to be out there dancing. I know that I am carrying on my traditions. I dance for my family and my tribe. The colors I use in my outfit, red, white, black, and

Left: Crows wear many large ankle bells and a string or two of leg bells. They carry dance sticks and mirror bags, paint their faces, and wear cloth capes, aprons, and hair pipe breastplates. Instead of wearing large bustles, they use small "feather duster" or natural feather bustles.

Below: Champion Crow dancer Walter Old Elk smiles while watching a contest. The Crows are renowned for Crow Fair, the largest outdoor powwow on the North American continent, which takes place annually on the third weekend in August. This event features daily parades and attracts 10,000 to 15,000 visitors and participants.

yellow, are the four natural colors of the land and the people who inhabit it. My dance clothes are a commitment to who I am and the people I associate with. The animal hides and headdress I wear signifies my Indian name, Powerful Walking Wolf."

Father and son, Larry and Darcy Anaquod, are Ojibway-Assiniboine from Muspowpetung, Queppele Valley, Saskatchewan. The entire family dances; daughter Lori is a Fancy Shawl dancer, and

Like his father Larry, on the right, Darcy Anaquod is a renowned Traditional dancer. Anishinabe (formerly Ojibway) tribal members, they traveled from their home in Saskatchewan, Canada, to attend the Red Bottom Celebration in Frazer, Montana.

mother Denise is a Traditional Jingle Dress dancer.

Larry began dancing as a little boy but quit in his twenties to "become an urban Indian and go rodeoing." Twenty years ago, he began dancing again as a Traditional dancer when his brother, Glen, a member of the River Bottom Singers, encouraged him to start.

The Anaquod family travels to more than thirty powwows a year in both Canada and the United States. "Several years ago we traveled with seventeen other singers and dancers as friendship representatives of Saskatchewan to Germany, Austria, and Switzerland. We were well-received and in the course of our performances were able to dispel the misconception of Indians as drinkers who constantly need babysitting," said Larry. "Many Europeans had this incorrect notion of native people. We became a major attraction in Germany and Austria where a scheduled half-hour performance would effortlessly stretch into two-and-a-half hours and the crowd of spectators would grow from four hundred to over a thousand. We felt like rock stars," Larry said.

Larry adds, "Drugs and alcohol don't mix with expressing our native culture. They are a big turn-off. The powwow is a big family circle where we have long-time friendships and we take care of each other." Darcy added, "I have been dancing since I could walk. I would get out in the center of the dance floor back then and now I continue to dance there. I've made that a trademark."

The Anaquods point out, "You'll never get rich participating in powwows. The expenses in dance clothes and traveling are too high." But it is not monetary rewards they seek. "You make lots of friends at powwows. That is the important thing. Those friendships are the riches one gets. Friends. We make new ones and meet again old ones. I've been able to take my kids all over the country. We travel, see, and enjoy the world. Without the powwow we wouldn't be doing that," he concludes. ⌘

Kevin Haywahe, Assiniboine, is almost entirely covered in ornate beadwork as he carries the Canadian flag in a Grand Entry at the Red Bottom Celebration. The red, yellow, white, and black in Kevin's regalia represent the four natural colors of the earth and the races who inhabit it.

Above: A lineup of teen Grass dancers at Browning, Montana.

Right: Three men's dance styles are present in this photograph. Left to right are Traditional, Southern Fancy, and Grass.

Facing page: Grass dancer "Big Wind" Windy Boy, Chippewa / Cree.

Above: *Jingle Dress dancers enter the dance circle at Rocky Boy.*

Facing page: *Champion Traditional dancer, Tim Eashappie, Sr., Assiniboine, is known for his athletic moves and stamina during contests. He trains constantly to stay in shape having developed a workout routine for dancers which he plans to put on video. He is rarely seen without his trademark sunglasses.*

PART 3
A CIRCLE OF EVENTS

Powwows usually run three to four days, starting with a camping day on Thursday, and lasting through Sunday. Other than socializing, the main activity at powwows is dancing. Powwows starting as early as Thursday will only have local people and early arrivals dancing. As visitors come, crowds swell with both spectators and participants. The Red Bottom Celebration (June) at Frazer, Montana, hosts a special Youth Powwow dedicated to, and run by, young people on Thursday night.

There are usually four to five Grand Entries over the weekend, with the first Friday night, two on Saturday, and one or two on Sunday. The final competitions for the adult categories take place on Sunday. When activities run late, the finals can take place early Monday morning. On those occasions the spectators are primarily friends, relatives and dancers huddling in blankets awaiting the results. All the tourists and casual spectators are gone, with a hard core few who stay up being rewarded with the day's best dancing and singing.

The three general kinds of dancing are intertribal dancing, contest dancing, and social dancing. Intertribal dances are best described by the announcer, "Everyone, get out on the floor and dance!" Since the participants are made up of all tribes present and all dance categories, ages, and genders, these dances are referred to as *intertribal*. "Shake those feathers, get off your duffs! Limber up and come out here and enjoy this good music!" Enjoying the music is the key to intertribal dancing. "You don't always have to be in regalia to dance an intertribal. You just have feel moved to come out here and have a good time."

Dance contests are broken down by categories, age, and gender. For example, there is men's Traditional, women's Fancy Shawl, teens' and boys' Grass, or girls seven to twelve years of age Jingle Dress.

Judges mark their ballots in descending order first through fifth, and points are awarded for placement in the preliminary sessions. Points are given for each participation in the Grand Entry. At the end of the powwow, these are tabulated to determine the finalists, and then a last contest session determines the winners. Most dancers compete in at least three sessions before being selected for finals.

Specials are dance arbor events that take place between the intertribal and contest sessions. These can be dance-oriented events like exhibitions or special contests, or honoring events like naming ceremonies, giveaways, and honor dances.

The main dance sessions start with a Grand Entry, flag ceremonies, prayers, blessings, and introductions of visiting dignitaries and royalty. The Grand Entry is exciting, spectacular and often spectators' favorite event of the powwow. The Grand Entry is a parade of dancers into the dance arbor. Men, women, and children enter by category of dance style with the oldest coming first, followed by the younger ones. Since elders lead the Grand Entry, the circle is completed when the youngest generation enters the arena. As dancers enter, the circle winds into itself and the center until everyone is in the arena. At major powwows, a Grand Entry can last over an hour with host drum groups taking turns singing. It is extremely enjoyable to watch a Grand Entry because you see all the different dance categories. You can pick out your favorite dance regalia and dancers and compare them to others.

Leading the parade of dancers are flag bearers who carry national, state, tribal, and veterans' organization flags. The prominent flag of the Grand Entry and the entire powwow is the Indian flag. This

Above: Tom Christian, Sioux, takes a break with the moon over his shoulder at Fort Belknap. A top Traditional dancer, he carefully coordinates the colors of his regalia. Top dancers keep abreast of fads and trends if they are to stay competitive. Many try to have new or different beadwork or make major modifications to their outfits on a regular basis.

Page 66: *The concentration of the judges is apparent as they choose winners in a young boys' Grass dance contest in Heart Butte, Montana.*

Canadian Roy Bison typifies the Northern Fancy dancer, wearing lots of fringe, heavy beadwork, and shaggier hackle feather bustles. Southern Fancy dancers sport a neater, tidier look, and their bustle hackle feathers are usually tied all facing the same direction.

Traditional dancers ring their bells in time to a Victory Song during a Grand Entry ceremony at Rocky Boy.

flag is usually a specially constructed crooked staff decorated with eagle feathers, beadwork, and buffalo fur. The flag symbolizes Indian people everywhere and is secured in a place of honor within the arena.

Flags can also be carried by formal color guards consisting of military veterans. Color guards, like the Northern Cheyenne Color Guard, practice and rehearse routines combining precision military drill with traditional tribal influences. During Lame Deer,

Above: These members of the Blackfeet Nation wear beaded buckskins and warbonnets. Such outfits are worn by respected elders and, though popularized by the movies, they are not commonly seen at powwow events.

Facing page: Many Jingle Dress dancers braid their hair in an intricate manner such as this young woman at North American Indian Days.

Montana's 1996 Fourth of July celebration, I was particularly lucky to observe the Cheyenne Victory Song and Dance. This ceremony, with its celebratory rifle firing, originated after the Battle of the Little Big Horn and the defeat of George Custer.

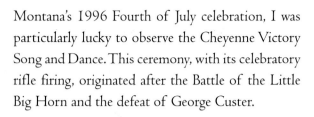

Once the dancers have paraded onto the dance floor and the flags are posted, respected elders of host and visiting tribes call upon the Creator. "Bless those who have traveled so far to be with us and help everyone here enjoy the powwow and have a safe trip home." Dignitaries are introduced following this blessing. These honored people can range from tribal chairpersons to respected veterans to distinguished college graduates. After the dignitaries, the announcers introduce the attending royalty.

Royalty are referred to as princesses. They are young girls ranging in age from toddlers to early womanhood. They distinguish themselves by participating in their culture, serving on powwow committees, or in some way earning the honor to represent their tribes. Beaded crowns and satin sash proclaim their title. Titles have names like Young Miss Fort Belknap, Northern Cheyenne Princess, Miss Blackfeet, or Rocky Boy Senior Princess. Once the opening ceremonies take place, the host drum sings the first intertribal song. The floor is at its most crowded as dancers "warm up to a good one."

Early in the powwow, there are many intertribals. For instance, on a Friday night most of the dancing may be all intertribal. As the powwow progresses over the weekend, special activities and contest sessions

Shari Daniels is ready for the women's Grass dance event having borrowed an excellent outfit.

take precedence and the number of intertribals will be reduced. These activities can be honor dances and songs, giveaways, exhibitions, and "specials."

Besides the regularly scheduled contests, various families can also sponsor special contests to honor a person or event. These family-sponsored contests are sometimes referred to as "winner takes all," or offer a special prize for the winner. The prize may take the form of cash, a trophy, a blanket, or a horse and saddle. Depending on the family's choice, these special contests can be any category. For instance, a family might honor their grandparents or children by sponsoring a "$500 winner take all" boys Fancy contest. As the contest progresses, the three finalists may offer to break the prize money into three equal increments or receive graduated amounts for first, second, and third place.

Specialty contests can also take the form of novelty dance contests. Twenty years ago, men's Fancy Shawl was a powwow highlight. Today, men's Jingle Dress is a crowd-pleaser on the northern powwow circuit. In this dance, men dress as women and compete in Jingle Dress outfits. Some men do their best to be convincing and faithfully emulate a female. They not only wear dresses, but also wear princess crowns, eye shadow and makeup, fully playing the part of a woman. Other male dancers become clowns enlarging their busts and buns with balloons and spoof the Jingle Dress style. Joking and playing with the audience, they attract attention any way they can. Pepsi Cola, which is popular in Indian country, also has the dubious distinction of having its cans rolled into jingles for clown dancers' Jingle Dress outfits.

These three Men's Jingle Dress dancers camp it up for the camera indicating their approach to the contest they are about to enter. While some males clown around in this unique men's contest, others go out of their way to be totally convincing as women.

The reverse of men's Jingle Dress is women's

Southern Traditional women enter the arbor at Rocky Boy's Powwow. They are differentiated from the Northern Women's Traditional by the lack of heavy beaded dress tops, their meticulously manicured outfits, and the fact that many dancers wear beaded crowns.

Grass dance. Contrary to some men who spoof the women's dance style, women usually take dancing women's Grass more seriously and will do their best to simulate and dance the style convincingly. Spectators sometimes have to look carefully to assure themselves these are women and not men.

Interspersed between dance contests and intertribals are honor dances, giveaways, and exhibitions. Exhibitions may be a contest category or a cultural presentation. When the announcer says, "All you dancers in the men's Grass dance get out there. We want to see you put on a show," dancers and audience members know it's an exhibition. Other exhibition dances may be specialty dances, the most popular of which is the hoop dance. Dancers perform with a multitude of hoops making patterns, or dancing with them intricately on their arms and legs. Another kind of specialty exhibition dance is what I refer to as a culture dance. These dances may originate from other tribes or countries. Some of these are Indian like the Apache Mountain Spirit Dance, the Aztec Fire Dance from Mexico, Haidas from the Northwest Coast presenting potlatch songs or Senecas doing a stomp dance. They may be non-Indian intercultural presentations. Norwegian clog dancing, Scottish bagpiping, Polynesian belly dancing with grass skirts, or traditional Thai dancing have all been observed at powwows. Indians have an interest in the demonstration of native culture from whatever country it may be.

Powwows not only enjoy the differences of American Indian tribes but encourage cultural displays from around the world. Blackfeet Tribal Chairman Earl Old Person joins the audience-participation fun by dancing with a Polynesian dance troupe in Browning.

Honor dances also take place in the arbor. Honor dances are sung by a drum group selected to sing for the person or family being honored. Anyone wishing to show respect or a connection to the honoree joins in the family as they circle the dance floor. These honor songs may be honoring either a deceased person or a living one who has distinguished himself in some way. For example, graduation from a college or high school, receiving a national award, being selected as head dancer, etc. Many times a giveaway will follow the honor dance.

Giveaways are unique to Indian people. In Indian country it's as honorable to give away gifts as to receive them. In giveaways, families gather goods and present them to extended family, friends, acquain-

Serving visitors at a Jonathan Windy Boy family feed on Rocky Boy's powwow grounds.

tances, and total strangers. Items can range from simple goods like baskets of food and money to beaded Indian items, star quilts, Pendleton blankets, tipis, and horses. Families save up money and items for an entire year, stockpiling them in preparation for giveaway. Giveaways are impressive and lengthy when pickup trucks back into the arbor to pile tables high with goods and horses covered with dollar bills are led into the arena.

Spectators and participants are free to come and go during the dance sessions. Dancers may leave the arena to go find a friend, check on their camp or a concession, get a drink or something to eat. Sometimes dancers will go back to camp during a lull in the activities for a break, get some food, visit, nap, or just sit back and relax.

Food is a key part of powwowing, and usually, on Saturday and Sunday afternoons, the supper break is filled with announcements of feeds throughout the camp. A feed is usually sponsored as part of an honoring. It may take place in conjunction with a giveaway or by itself. Large family feeds take days to prepare with members preparing traditional foods like fry bread, tripe, berry soups, salmon, and more common foods like potato salads, hamburgers, or barbecued buffalo or beef. Large feeds can take place in the arbor or at campsites. Thanks to the concessions, ration distribution and feeds, there is no shortage of food at powwows. Eating together is an informal way of bonding and socializing. A powwow isn't a celebration without food. ✠

Winona Runsabove, Sioux / Cheyenne / Assiniboine, and Jaycene Windy Boy, Chippewa / Cree, share a special camaraderie having grown up in the powwow world.

Darrell Abrahamson, Colville, and Steve Small Salmon, Salish, have fun and entertain the spectators by sneaking up on the camera at North American Indian Days.

On hot days, an ice cream break is the way to go. This stand leaves little to the imagination as to what it offers.

PART 4

A CIRCLE OF LIFE

Just like the Plains tribes who followed the buffalo, powwow people tend to be nomadic. Some professional participants travel all year and some only use the summer months to travel hundreds of miles from powwow to powwow. While others, wishing they could be on the road, but having homebound responsibilities, are only able to attend one or two events a year. Even though they have differing degrees of participation, they are all powwow people due to their involvement and dedication to this age-old expression of native culture.

Entire families, from the youngest to the oldest, participate in powwows. They demonstrate their interest in many ways. While certain family members dance, others may sing at the drum. A lot of participants do both. Parents, grandparents, and siblings help each other get ready or work on outfits. Others, tired of the pace, take a powwow or an entire summer off to watch, visit, and relax without the pres-

sure of Grand Entries and contests.

Traditional powwows or non-contest powwows are gaining in popularity for both financial and social reasons. Since there are no contests to fund, these events are much less expensive for the sponsoring organization to host. Dancers and singers can enjoy the powwow and allow themselves to participate for the enjoyment of the dance itself.

Indian people do not perform when they dance. Dancing is engaged in for the benefit of the individual and the group as a whole. Many times during the weekend, announcers will thank the dancers "for being out there on the floor and helping us out." Participants are reaffirming their culture and strengthening a way of life which manifests itself in a most visible and affecting way. People of the circle dance and sing for each other, to ensure that life continues, and tribal and cultural ways are not lost. This spirit is both seen and felt. The energy it exudes is absorbed, and permeates throughout all the people present.

Powwow life not only exists for the most visible participants, but for many others, as well. All of those engaged in the powwow are affected in some way, whether they are hosts, visitors, participants, or spectators. Concessionaires and vendors also follow the powwow trail. They work their stands with limited

Above: *Powwow people help each other as Walter Old Elk demonstrates by helping these Jingle Dress dancers start their car at Lame Deer, Montana's Fourth of July Celebration. Walter's beaded dance set is recognizably Crow and was a gift from his sons.*

Page 78: *An elder shows his appreciation for the good time he is having at Rocky Boy's Memorial Powwow. He asks a blessing on all the people present and wishes everyone a safe trip home.*

sleep, working in all kinds of conditions. Heat, cold, wind, dust, rain, mud, and insects, all take their toll. Rest and relaxation doesn't arrive on the weekend, but hopefully comes between events. But only if the next event is close and travel isn't extensive.

Because of their popularity and demand on the circuit, some people never stop. They just occasionally slow down. These powwow luminaries may be in Florida one weekend and in Washington state the next. Most drive the distance in well-used vehicles, stopping at friends' homes to spend nights along the way. A fortunate few, seasoned veterans are able to request plane tickets, motel accommodations and expenses.

Worlds apart, but together within the circle, Rocky Boy's Reservation powwow and the urban, high-tech Schemitzun in Connecticut are events that exist at either end of the powwow life continuum.

One is the elder, steeped in traditional ways while the other is young, fresh, and flush with "new buffalo" riches. It is a member of the new generation of powwows. Both are popular and attract many participants and spectators.

They are a good examples of the broad differences and similarities that exist for people who make the powwow part of their life.

ROCKY BOY'S MEMORIAL POWWOW

"Good morning, Indian America! Roll over, you sleepy Indians, let's shake a few feathers," boomed the voice over the public address system. Reenacting an age-old tradition, the camp crier, Russell Standing Rock, awoke the encampment with announcements of the day's scheduled events.

People were already up and about, the smell of

A view from the hill looking down on the 1996 Rocky Boy's Memorial Powwow. The cooling shade trees on the arbor and campsites are box elder branches and saplings which are cut by the truckload in the foothills of the Bears Paw Mountains and positioned just before the powwow starts. Note the mixture of recreational vehicles, tents and tipis which dot the grounds.

Not all Crows dance Traditional. Christian Takes Gun is quick, light, wiry, and nimble—physical assets that suit him well as a Fancy dancer.

smoke and fresh coffee mingling in the air. It was time to roll out and start the day.

My family and I had arrived late the previous afternoon following a hot five-hour drive from Missoula. It was the first weekend in August and time for the Rocky Boy's Memorial Powwow and Celebration.

It isn't only the land that changes when you turn off U.S. Highway 87 and head onto the reservation. Barren, stubbled wheatfields give way to rolling foothills, meandering streams, shimmering box elder groves, and the forested canyons of the Bear Paw Mountains. Air conditioned combines are replaced by browsing horses and free roaming cattle. Homes have tipi poles stacked against them, old cars and an occasional sweat lodge dot the yards. An ancient people, rich with tradition inhabit this land. We are in Chippewa-Cree country.

Pulling into camp, "Uncle" Kenny Standing

Rock said, "It's about time you got here, bro'. I saved you a place but the camp is filling fast. I was afraid I was going to have to get a new barbecue cook for tomorrow's feed, but I see you made it." "Come over and eat after you get that tent up," his sister Harriet says. "I gotta get 'Chief', he's over at the arbor drum hopping and Dody needs to get dressed for Grand Entry." She hurries off after her children. Her husband, Earl Arkinson, is at work. Earl is tribal chief of police and this is the busiest weekend of the year.

We were surprised by the size of the camp. Last year's attendance was down. But 1996's event was Rocky Boy as usual. People had come from all over the United States and Canada. Even representatives of East coast tribes were in attendance. A brown haze of dust and smoke hung over the 3,000 people preparing for the evening's dance. Tipis, tents, cars, trucks and campers were spread everywhere.

Nestled in the foothills of the Bears Paw Moun-

Oklahoman Ralph Haymond, Jr., Pawnee/Otoe, shows the concentration and focus it takes to be a champion Southern Straight dancer.

Above: Evan Melting Tallow, Blood, a good and noble man, who is missed by those who knew and loved him, at 1993's Heart Butte Celebration.

Right: A full beaded porcupine roach spreader at Seattle's Il-Wa-Sil Powwow.

tains and extending north toward old Fort Assiniboine, Rocky Boy's Reservation was the last one to be officially established in Montana in September 1916. The Memorial Powwow was launched in 1964 to commemorate the fiftieth anniversary of establishing this Chippewa-Cree homeland. Since then, this celebration has grown to be one of the largest and more popular powwows in the United States. It is not uncommon to encounter over 1,500 participants at this event, though non-Indian tourist spectators are sparse due to the reservation's remote location.

Like many others, Rocky Boy's Reservation has two resident tribes, bands of both Chippewa and Cree. Many historians believe that the Chippewa, led by Chief Stone Child, arrived from the Turtle Mountain region of North Dakota after 1875. The Cree were members of Little Bear's wandering band that left Canada in 1885 during the Riel Rebellion. For more than twenty years, the two bands roamed the state, unable to find a place to settle.

Stone Child actively pursued a homeland. Government officials, misunderstanding the translation of his name, referred to him as "Rocky Boy" and the name stuck. The chief died six months before President Woodrow Wilson signed the order creating Rocky Boy's Reservation.

As of October 1994, tribal enrollment records listed 4,713 members, about 40 percent of whom

Jingle dresses come in a wide assortment of patterns. This one was at Kamiah, Idaho, in Nez Perce country.

Above: One young dancer is lost in her scissortail fan while her taller comrades have their numbers taken after a contest.

Facing page: Fancy dancer Larry Yazzie.

live off the reservation. Regardless of strict tribal enrollment policies, population projections show that there may be as many as 9,300 members residing on the reservation by 2020. The land holdings have grown from 55,040 acres to approximately 121,000 acres. Even though the reservation has grown 11 percent in the last decade, Rocky Boy's has always suffered from too little land to adequately support its population.

A force behind the first Rocky Boy's Powwow over thirty years ago was Florence Standing Rock, granddaughter of Cree Chief Little Bear. The Standing Rock family continues to be an integral part of the reservation community and powwow.

"We're a very poor reservation," Russell Standing Rock comments, "but we have a reputation as a people of hospitality. That's why this is one of the major powwows in the nation. Ours is also more traditional than most. We give out rations, host lots of feeds, our giveaways are famous, and we always have many special contests for the participants. We are one of the few northern tribes to present Southern Straight contests. The last couple of years, we've had several Grass Dance specials where there are over 100

Grass dancers on the floor, and our Crow Belt special gets larger every year." He adds, "We're off the main highways, and visitors have to go out of their way to visit us. We want them to feel welcome."

□

"One of the hardest jobs in the powwow world is judging dancers," declares Canadian elder Alex Scalplock. "Few people understand how difficult it is to give or take points away from a dancer. The most common mistake is being out of beat with the drum. Many judges don't think it is important. They look for fancy moves. But it's the most important thing, to have a good rhythm and move your entire body in time with the drum," says Scalplock who is a frequent judge at powwows.

Above: Face paint can be an important element of a Traditional dancer's decoration. Care has to be taken in its application to insure evenness and coverage. Some dancers have a trademark face paint design while others will change their design from session to session. Face paint is more commonly seen during the cooler night sessions and is definitely worn to help make a difference in final contests.

Top: Parents introduce their children to the powwow world early in life. U-Lath-Quin-Sit, Lummi, from Washington, shades his family from the sun at the Bitterroot Good Nations Powwow.

Teenager Carol Melting Tallow, Blood, dons an eagle feather visor and wings to add effect to her Fancy Shawl outfit in Heart Butte, Montana. Large amounts of eagle feathers are not commonly seen on women. Indian women's traditional roles have been affected by modern society. Just like the everyday world, the powwow world observes changes as roles evolve.

"The drummers try to confuse the dancer, but really good dancers know the song and are not tricked because they listen to the beat," says Scalplock. "In Fancy dance, for instance, trick songs may be introduced to catch the dancers off guard. There may be a ruffle, a shake, a sneak-up, or a Crow hop. Sometimes songs have lots of stops in them. A dancer must be ready in order not to get caught," he adds.

In addition to contests and intertribal dances, other events take place at the Rocky Boy's Powwow. There are exhibition dances, gourd dances, hand drum singing demonstrations, Native American Church events, name-givings and adoptions. The tribe hosts a foot race, a softball tournament, and a rodeo.

The Rocky Boy's Powwow grounds are adjacent to the location of the Sun Dance held a month earlier. Those bough-bedecked arbors stand vigilantly across a gully from the encampment area. Bright pieces of cloth flap and wave colorfully in the afternoon breezes. According to Derek Small, "The Sun Dance lodges are left standing to continue bringing the blessings and power of the Sun Dance to the community. The Chippewa-Cree of Rocky Boy do not separate the sacred and the secular, but incorporate both into their lives."

Alvin Windy Boy sums up the Chippewa-Cree philosophy when he points out that powwow people are not short-sighted. "There is no line drawn. We are all in this world and must share it together. There is more to the powwow than the version seen in the media. We do not look upon the powwow as a sideshow. We are not providing a pageant or entertainment. We are interpreting an Indian awareness by incorporating spiritual and cultural aspects into this enriching event."

SCHEMITZUN—THE WORLD CHAMPIONSHIP OF SINGING AND DANCE

Excitement fills the air as the house lights slowly fade. The noisy arena hushes. $200,000 in prize money and a production cost of $2.5 million truly makes this "World Championship of Singing and Dance" the richest powwow in history, and everyone is anxious.

The air-conditioned, temperature controlled Hartford Civic Center Arena is huge. It has a capacity of 15,000 plush seats. The immense floor is covered with brand new gray pile industrial carpeting.

Most of the participants are hundreds of miles from their homelands and far from Indian country. Over 700 dancers made their way into the dance circle on that first day in September 1993. That number more than doubled to 1,500 by the weekend. The amount of spectators grew daily until over 20,000 people would attend the event over four days. I was attending Schemitzun as a guest of the Mashantucket Pequot tribe in the capacity of staff photographer. I was also able to dance in my first men's Golden Age at the ripe old age of forty-five.

This blend of culture and professional presentation is typical of how the wealthy Pequot Tribe hosts Schemitzun in Hartford, Connecticut, the state capital. "Schemitzun," (pronounced ska-MIT-zun), translates as "Feast of Green Corn and Dance" in the Pequot language.

The Pequots' concern for reviving their tradi-

Though the powwow originated as a plains cultural phenomenon, it has spread throughout Indian country. Nanepashemet, who was working at the Plimouth Plantation in Massachusetts, shows his Eastern tribal origins with his shaved head at Schemitzun '93.

John Windy Boy, Chippewa-Cree, on the dance floor at the 1993 Schemitzun, the year he won the Boys Fancy Dance division.

tions and providing motivation for young New England Indians to take pride in their culture prompted them to produce Schemitzun. Schemitzun harkens to an historic harvest celebration originally celebrated just as the first ears of corn ripened.

For centuries the Mohegan-Pequot lands stretched across what is now southeastern Connecticut. English and Dutch settlers arrived in the early 1600s. It is estimated there were 3,000 to 4,000 Pequots living in eight to ten villages at that time. Within two decades, smallpox and other diseases killed over half the population. On June 1, 1637, the colonists and Indian allies attacked the Pequots at Mystic Fort. In the ensuing massacre, hundreds of Pequots died. Many of the survivors were delivered into slavery.

An Indian flag posted by the speakers stand at Schemitzun '93.

For the next three centuries the Pequots struggled to regain their land and their tribal identity. Following years of negotiation and the help of the Native American Rights Fund the tribe was finally recognized by the U.S. government in 1983.

A bingo casino was opened in 1986 which eventually led to the development of Foxwoods Casino in February 1992. Foxwoods is one of the Western Hemisphere's largest casinos. Twenty-seven million people live within a 150-mile radius. They provide the casino with crowds that can reach 24,000 a day. The Mashantucket Pequot tribe established the Schemitzun powwow in the early 1990s in an effort to revive interest in their culture. They used some of their gaming profits and invited tribes from all over the continent to come and share in their new event.

Unlike other powwows, Schemitzun also offers a full slate of professional native entertainers: performing groups like Redbone, folk singer/actor Floyd Westerman, Keith Secola, Mixashaun, Curtis "Shingoose" Jonnie, and Joanne Shenandoah and Canada's Clyde Roulette Band.

It is time to head to the dance arena in the Civic Center. Many participants have chosen to stay in the Hartford Sheraton which is at the far end of an indoor shopping mall from the arena. By traveling on elevators and escalators, there is a five-minute "foot commute" from hotel rooms to the Civic Center.

Merle Tendoy, a singer with the Eagle Whistles drum group, asks if I have discovered the fitness room on the Sheraton's third floor. "It's great," he enthusiastically tells me. " It has a pool, hot tub, sauna, jacuzzi, and exercise equipment. Last night I decided to sweat in the sauna. There were a couple of Bloods from Canada who told me that 'the white man's sweat house is bigger than the sweat lodges back home but the rocks are too small and don't heat it enough. The more water we pour on 'em, the less heat we get.' Water was two inches deep on the floor. That sauna was 220 degrees at one hundred percent humidity. I broke a sweat in seconds."

Lead singers from twenty-seven drum groups participate in an honor song prior to the giveaway at the 1993 Schemitzun Powwow in the Hartford Civic Arena.

Fully dressed dancers are exiting rooms and the jangle of bells and jingle dresses mixes with hectic voices exhorting others to hurry. Down the hall the elevator dings its arrival. R.G. Harris, a well-known Fancy dancer, is a flurry of feathers as he rushes to halt the closing doors. "Watch the feathers! Watch the feathers," he says. He backs into the compartment opening a hole in the costumed crowd for his little ones. "See those two gray-suited, wide-eyed white guys in the corner?" he asks. I nod. "This is one business trip they'll never forget!"

Members of the Pequot tribe pose for a family picture. In the 1700s, many Pequots were removed from their ancestral lands. They were placed on plantations where they intermarried with African slaves. The combinations of these bloodlines are in evidence today as many members of the tribe draw from both an Indian and African-American cultural heritage.

Two floors down we pick up Tim White Eyes, a champion Traditional dancer. His "black and white" outfit is striking. His beadwork features black and white checks and is worn over a white and black striped shirt. A vertical white stripe from forehead to chin splits each side of his black-painted face. His dark-tipped eagle feather visor further shades his features affording him a menacing demeanor. His shoulders are broadened with horsehair-tipped feathered "wings." White buckskin leggings with long fringes and black stripes cover his legs. A painted rawhide shield is secured to his left arm. He holds a large eagle wing fan in one hand. His other hand brandishes a wicked ball-headed warclub embellished with beadwork, feathers, and scalplocks. "Hey Tim, you're dressed to kill," R.G. jokes. "Dang right, R.G.! I'm ready!" Tim answers. The two businessmen shrink further back into the elevator.

The elevator stops at each floor as we descend but is too full for more passengers. When we reach the third floor, the businessmen softly say, "This is our stop please. Our meeting is on this floor." As the doors open, their way out is blocked by another group of gray suits waiting to ride.

"Aieee...ah!" A piercing scream shatters the air. Tim springs forward, shaking his club and rattling his dewclaw kneebands. He clears the way as the suits jump back. One man meekly says, "Uhm...ah,

we'll take the next one, thanks." Our two departing passengers slink silently out as the doors slide together. A grin on his face, Tim chuckles, "Gotcha!" The elevator doors close. We all descend to the lobby, laughing.

Spectators on Sunday witnessed the awards for the dance and drum contests. The Pequots also hosted a giveaway by the Schemitzun festival committee. This giveaway featured an honor song sung by all lead singers present. Four hundred star quilts and Pendleton blankets were laid out, one overlapping another in a patchwork mosaic of color. Twenty-seven lead singers were seated around four drums. Slowly their mesmeric song built in majesty creating an inspiring moment. When the song ended, the Pequot tribe honored "those who helped us out" by calling numerous people to receive a blanket or quilt.

Jingle dress dancers enjoy the carpeted dance floor and air conditioning in the Hartford Civic Arena. In subsequent years, the celebration was moved to Ledyard, Connecticut, on the Pequot Reservation, but returned to Hartford in 1997 to better accommodate the large number of people who attend.

Oklahoma's champion Southern Style Fancy dancers R.G. Harris and Dwight White Buffalo "go around." R.G. and Dwight are good friends who compete against each other regularly. They travel from coast to coast during the course of a powwow season. In August they come north, attracted by the special Southern Fancy Dance contest at Rocky Boy's and the noted Chippewa/Cree hospitality. A month later they can usually be found in Hartford, Connecticut, at Schemitzun.

Two dynamic dancers definitely dueled it out in the Southern Fancy category. R.G. Harris, the older seasoned veteran, has been in his prime for many years, while Dwight White Buffalo, nimbly athletic, is the younger of the two. They battled for first and second place. As the contest progressed, R.G. slowed and was slightly less dramatic as Dwight "turned on the moves." Using spins and splits, pivots and back-pedals, fancy footwork and "flying mule kicks," each dancer gave his best effort. It wasn't until the final beat the contest was decided. Endings are an integral element of any performance. R.G. knew the song and stopped right on the beat, every muscle accentuating his final move. Dwight went for a fancier stop. The knee drop, a real winner with no room

for error. A fraction of a beat off and points are lost. We had to await the awards to know the result of this dance off.

"Ladies and Gentlemen! The winner of the men's Southern Fancy Dance...from the great state of Oklahoma...a respected champion...Number eleven-sixty-three...R.G. Harris!"

Dwight's timing had been off. He'd hit the floor with his knees a half beat too soon.

First-place winners in the adult categories received $2,000 and embroidered suede leather jackets. First-place winners in the Golden Age category were awarded $2,500 and jackets.

When the awards were over, the floor filled with festive dancers and singers for a champions honor song. Seven happy members of first place singing

Women Traditional dancer at Schemitzun. The woven hat on the woman on the left identifies her as being from a Columbia Basin Plateau tribe. As powwows proliferate around the continent, regional tribal influences are more readily apparent to the educated eye.

These two young Grass dancers were using up excess energy climbing on the roof supports of the dance pavilion at Fort Belknap, Montana. They kept saying, "Take our picture." So I did.

group, Alberta's own Stoney Park, stood in the center while countless fans took their picture. They would go home with $10,000 and suede jackets. "Now everyone here join these powwow champions for the final dance," the announcer said. "Color guard! Remove the flags. Please follow the flags as they exit the arena. We wish you all a safe trip home and thank you for being here. Good night, and may the Creator bless you all. Ah Ho!" 1993's Schemitzun was in the history books.

CHILDREN OF THE CIRCLE

The circle of life is endless. There is no beginning and no end. It continues on and on. We go from infant to child, adult to elder. Indian tribes compare these cycles of life to the four seasons. Winter is the time of old age. The snow on the ground is white, and so is the hair of elders. Autumn is adulthood. It is harvest time and just as the harvest provides sustenance for the earth's people, adults provide for the younger generation. Infants and children are spring and summer. Spring is birth. As shoots and seedlings promise new growth, infants are life reborn. Childhood is summer. What was born in spring, grows and matures in summer. Children become the people they will be as adults. As seasons are essential to life, all ages are needed to fill the powwow circle.

Children are a vital element of Indian life and powwows. Their presence and participation are an integral part of the celebration. With-

out children, a powwow would not be the event it is. These young participants ensure the continuation of songs, dances, traditional ways, an entire cultural heritage.

Indian children are taught to respect those who are older and wiser than they. They are taught that

Shaylon Gopher, Blackfeet/Chippewa/Cree/Jemez Pueblo, showing his contest winning Grass dance abilities at North American Indian Days.

any close adult, whether they be blood relation or not, is honored as either aunt, uncle, mother, father, or grandparent. Children look to adults for guidance, while adults look to children as new life and future promise. They value children because they know if traditions are to continue the young must learn and carry on those traditions. Children are encouraged. They are not pushed. They are allowed to be children, not shoved into adulthood. Children are led into cultural ways through family participation. If parents participate in powwows and involve themselves in their native culture, children will learn by example.

Francis and Louann Kicking Woman both dance and so do their children. Francis is a Blackfeet Traditional dancer who met his Assiniboine wife on the Fort Peck Reservation in Montana. When Francis was young, he moved off the reservation and his family now lives in Missoula. He and Louann are raising their children with the powwow and cultural ways as part of their lives. Like most powwow parents, they encourage their children by example.

"My kids dance when they want to. I don't push them or throw them into the dance arena. I see some parents grabbing and shaking their kids to go and dance. My dad didn't make me dance. I was seventeen and sitting back at Browning Indian Days watching all my cousins and friends dancing. I got lonely sitting there all by myself watching them having a

good time. I ran home and told my dad and mom I wanted to dance. They went right out the next day and bought things for an outfit. They got Hong Kong beadwork and slapped it together that day. It wasn't really Grass, Fancy, or Traditional, it was just an outfit. I didn't even have a headdress," Francis said.

"When I went out on the dance floor, I was kinda scared," he continued. "I wasn't used to the crowd watching me. When my friends saw me they were proud I wanted to dance. They surrounded me and

Above: Two young Fancy Shawl dancers beam with pride at Arlee, Montana, during their annual Fourth of July Celebration. This powwow will celebrate its 100th Anniversary in 1998. The girl's hair ties on the left are made of both porcupine quillwork combined with beadwork. The use of quillwork is seeing a resurgence on the Northern Plains.

Facing page: This young Grass dancer stops briefly by a tipi on his way to an evening Grand Entry at Fort Belknap.

put me in the middle and danced me around the floor for a while, and then, all of a sudden, they were gone and I was by myself. They said I was trained. Since that day, I've danced Fancy or Traditional for the past eighteen years."

Some traditions start because of young people. According to an Ojibwe story the Jingle Dress dance originated this way. "Many years ago a daughter, who was dearly loved by her father, became very ill and lay dying. The father prayed and prayed for her to get well. One night in a dream, a woman appeared to him. In his dream the woman showed the father how to make a jingle dress. In the dream the father heard jingle dress songs while the woman danced. When he awoke he told his wife about the dream. They decided to make a jingle dress and teach their daughter how to dance this new style. Then they had their daughter wear the dress and dance to the songs her father had taught his singers. The girl got well." This dance then spread through the tribe. It is said the Ojibwe then passed this dance on to other tribes. Today the Jingle Dress dance is very popular and continues to spread throughout the continent.

Above: *Just like adults, children on the powwow circuit make friends and constantly renew old acquaintances. Shaylon Gopher and his Fancy dancer friend were visiting between dance sessions at Rocky Boy's August powwow.*

Facing page: *A happy little participant at Rocky Boy's powwow.*

Right: Kyle Sam's father, Richard Rock, is also a Grass dancer.

Below: Two good friends are happy to pose for the camera at Fort Belknap demonstrating the spirit of youth who are involved in the powwow world.

Facing page: Andrea "Sissy" Gopher, Blackfeet / Chippewa / Cree / Jemez Pueblo, younger sister of Shaylon Gopher, shows her contest winning Jingle Dress style at North American Indian Days in Browning, Montana.

WOMEN OF THE CIRCLE

"My northern grandmother told me the story of how the Northern Fancy Shawl dance came about," says Bonnie Tomahsah, a talented Comanche fancy shawl dancer. "According to legend, butterfly lost her mate. He had been killed and she was very sad. So she went into her cocoon to mourn. When she came out of her cocoon she started dancing to release her feelings. The more she danced the better she felt and soon she was free of her sadness."

Above: *Lucy Finley shows her enjoyment with the Standing Arrow Powwow at Elmo, Montana.*

Facing page: *Rose Ann Abrahamson, a Lemhi Shoshone from Fort Hall, Idaho, exudes the dignity and grace of a Traditional dancer at Rocky Boy.*

Just like that legend of old, an ever-increasing number of Indian women are coming out of their cocoons on the powwow dance floor and in society in general. As women's roles have changed in today's world, so they are changing in the powwow world. Women's traditional roles have been affected by modern society. As women change their function in the expression of their culture so do their roles change within the entire culture. Women's changing role in the powwow crosses over to Indian society in general. Women are becoming more noticeable and taking on more responsibility in both powwows and tribal government.

Today we see women tribal council members and chairpersons. This is ongoing and evolving. Change is continually taking place. The powwow circuit, which has primarily been dominated by male personalities, now also has well-known and esteemed female ones.

As recently as twenty-five years ago, women at Northern Plains powwows traditionally sang in a high falsetto in a supporting role behind male drummers. They rarely sat at the drum or used drumsticks with the men. Today it is not unusual for women (and children) to sit at the drum and sing with men. Rae Lynn Kicking Woman (Blackfeet) often leads off songs for the popular Kicking Woman Singers. This change has extended even further in the past few years. Though they initially created a stir and definitely drew attention, the Crying Woman all woman drum group led by female lead singers from Fort Belknap, Montana, found acceptance and respect on the circuit.

Above: The artistry of Douglas Standing Rock, Chippewa/Cree, is readily apparent in a scene he created in beads for the Traditional dress worn by his daughter, Paulette. Douglas is a well known painter who works for the tribe and beads his family's dance clothes. Many Rocky Boy people are active in the Native American Church. Douglas has incorporated design motifs from his background into this beautiful example of contemporary beadwork.

Facing page: Cora Chandler, a Gros Ventre Fancy Shawl dancer, seems to float above the ground at the Fourth of July Celebration in Lame Deer, Montana. The shawl she wears is said to represent the wings of a butterfly.

"To be able to do this just like the men is a big opportunity for women," says Bonnie Tomahsah. "To be able to show the men that we can do this is important." Bonnie's comments are part of the American Indian Dance Theatre's most recent PBS-television production entitled *Dances for the New Generations.*

Tomahsah and a group of young women dancers are on camera discussing what dancing means to them and the roles they play in powwows.

Powwow dancing as we know it today evolved from religious and social dances of the plains tribes. Both northern and southern plains tribes depended on the land for their food, clothing and shelter. If they stayed in large groups they overly taxed "Mother Earth," so they split into smaller bands and family groups. Once or twice a year, they would gather to renew allegiances and conduct tribal ceremonies. The ceremonies often involved feasting, dancing, and socializing. During the winter, when activity was limited the people had time to decorate special clothing for the summer's reunion. These summer reunions took place at prearranged locations and dates. All tribal members gathered for social

Christian religious elements are pronounced in this outstanding beaded contemporary Traditional dress at Browning, Montana. The theme of this dress is carried out magnificently from head to toe. A dress such us this can weigh as much as forty pounds.

activities and religious ceremonies that reaffirmed their unity. During this time clans and societies held their annual rites. As in the past, cultural traditions continue to strengthen at these gatherings which continue in the form of powwows or "Indian celebrations."

And these traditions are evolving. Joni Lamb, Gros Ventre, is both a prize-winning Jingle Dress dancer and president of the University of Montana's American Indian Business Leaders (AIBL) chapter. She points out, "Women's roles in the powwow circle have evolved with society. We have taken strides towards equality with our male counterparts. Today, women are awarded the same prize money as the men in the dance competitions. Fancy Shawl dancing is as exciting as Men's Fancy. Jingle Dress dancing is so popular that dancers fill the dance floor during contests. In many tribes we are now seeing all women's drum groups or women leading the men. We are also now seeing more women rising to prominence in the cultural arena."

Rosalie Jones, Blackfeet/Cree, professor of dance at Santa Fe's Institute of American Indian Arts and artistic founder of the interpretive Daystar Dance Company, believes there is a lot of untapped talent in Indian country. In promotional literature for the Institute she says, "One way to develop this talent is to introduce people from different tribes to dance and theater. In turn they will teach what they have learned to the youth of tomorrow." She believes there is a wealth of traditional lore and culture that can be used through dance to educate the public. "American Indian people have volumes to speak, not only to non-Indian society, but to each other as well. I feel we can all benefit from Indian philosophy and life experience." Professor Jones goes on to say that she intends to be "a catalyst for cross-cultural understanding" through her role as a performer, teacher, and choreographer.

Maggie Black Kettle, a respected Canadian elder, is a familiar face on both sides of the border.

Participation in powwows assists in combating drug and alcohol abuse. Since powwows are family events, the use of intoxicants is frowned upon and strong measures are taken to insure that alcohol is not present on the grounds. The message on this young Jingle dancer encourages others to avoid the dangers.

Jingle Dress dancers line up for the judges after a dance contest.

An example of a young Indian woman who has benefited from the cultural awareness and knowledge she learned in the powwow dance circle is Crystal Pewo. Miss Pewo, a twenty-year-old Kiowa/Apache, was the 1995 Miss Indian World, a title she won at the Gathering of Nations powwow in Albuquerque, New Mexico. Many of Pewo's traditional native ways were taught to her by her grandparents. "I learned a lot from my granny...how to bead...she spoke four languages, Kiowa, Comanche, Apache, and English.

"I started dancing when I was two, and became real involved around the age of ten. Then I was old enough to travel with my grandparents and they took me all over." She is also thankful to her parents for all the support and encouragement she received in getting a good education. "I was real lucky. I had a lot more opportunity than other kids had." Before competing for the Miss Indian World crown, Crystal had experience as a princess for a southern drum group and her high school Indian club. "Competing in the Junior Miss Indian Oklahoma pageant helped me grow a lot more. I knew what to expect. But when I walked into the room and saw twenty-one other talented contestants I wanted to turn around and walk out."

Pewo called upon her dancing and her public speaking skills to win the title. She performed a Southern traditional dance and sang a Kiowa prayer song she had learned in church, embellishing it with sign language.

Because of her celebrity status she was asked to attend the Paul Band Powwow west of Edmonton, Alberta, Canada. "I was invited because their chief, Rema Rain, is female and the committee wanted to do something different and have me give a short talk on women's roles and leadership. It really touched me. While I was there little girls came up to me and talked to me like I was a goddess or something."

Since entering college as an industrial engineering major she has been thinking increasingly about using her talents at the community level. She finds herself looking inward to her culture and envisions herself working more with her own people, especially youth. Pewo knows she can make a difference.

In the past twenty years or so, a number of Indian women have established themselves as leaders in both the cultural realm and in political circles as well. By the 1980s, women headed more than ten percent of the United States' tribal councils. According to Time-Life Books, twenty-two of California's tribal groups were governed by women. As politicians, women address contemporary problems while drawing inspiration from the past and serving as guardians of their people's heritage.

Alta Swiftbird, a Sioux from South Dakota, wears a dentalium shell breastplate over her dress.

One woman who achieved political prominence by reaffirming her ties to her Cherokee people and their traditions is Wilma Mankiller. In 1985, she became principal chief of the Cherokee. She won re-election twice to that post, most recently in 1991, when she received endorsement by nearly 83 percent of Cherokee voters.

In a recent essay she wrote, "When I walked through the door of the Cherokee Nation offices in 1976 looking for a job, I never dreamed I would someday have the honor and the privilege of leading the second largest tribe in North America. At that time, there were no female executives in the tribe; there had not been a female deputy chief or a female principal chief. My becoming chief was not part of a strategy. It was my being in the right place at the right time, combined with my own willingness to take a risk. It has been said that I like to dance along the edge of a roof.

"My being female made the elections that much more difficult. Women learn to deal with overt gender-based opposition in different ways. In my case, I chose to ignore the opposition and remain focused on the issues. In the old days, the Cherokee people believed the world existed in a precarious balance and only right or correct actions kept it from tumbling. Wrong actions were believed to disturb balance. In my view gender balance in leadership is very important to all people. The viewpoint of men is important in all areas of society, as is the viewpoint of women."

More now than ever before, the women of the circle play a role in shaping, strengthening and enriching American Indian culture.

Women's roles have changed in the powwow world. Thirty years ago, women usually sang behind the drum and rarely touched a drumstick. Today, women not only sing at the drum but lead off songs. Fancy Shawl dancer Patty Young Running Crane, Blackfeet, "helps out" with the Kicking Woman Singers, comprised of both males and females.

These women at Schemitzun are wearing the star quilts they received in the giveaway. The lady on the left is a Southern Style Traditional dancer and the woman in the center is a Northern Style.

Allen Slickpoo, Nez Perce, is glad to encounter Sunny Tuttle, Sioux, whom he hasn't seen for many years at the United Peoples Powwow in Missoula, Montana. Socializing is one of the most important functions of a powwow. Both cultural and personal friendship bonds are reaffirmed. Allen is wearing an old style split horned bonnet while Sunny wears the more common porcupine roach.

Powwow life ingrains itself into the very makeup of a person. Once truly experienced, it is not easily put aside. It's a fact of that life and applies to Indian and non-Indian alike. Non-Indians become involved in powwows in a variety of ways, though few have the time and dedication to become dancers or singers. Many are food or trade vendors. Others serve on committees, assist with security or first aid, or help with fund raising. Several years ago an entire non-Indian community in the Wallowa Valley of Oregon hosted a celebration to honor the Nez Perce tribe. Like other newly established events, this celebration continues to grow. Inter-culturalism is a way of powwow life and respectful non-Indians are welcome and appreciated.

Many times, I'm asked by puzzled non-Indians about my involvement in powwows. "How are you accepted?" they ask. "Like any other person," is my reply. "Though with a bit more curiosity by those who don't know me," I sometimes add.

I have always been made welcome. After thirty-three years in powwow country my family and I are proud and fortunate to have many well-respected powwow people as friends and relations. My children have wonderful "aunties and uncles" who encourage them to dance, sing, play, visit, eat; to be part of their life, too. Though we are not Indian, we try our best to learn Indian ways and respect them. With that knowledge and the acceptance of the fact that everyone in the world is different, we are able to

Right: Adolescent behavior manifests itself at Lame Deer, Montana, just as it would in the city. Here, basketball players take a break to visit with two sisters who are on a break also. Dancing at powwows can be as demanding as any sport and bears a lot of similarity to competitive athletic events. They both need the prerequisite equipment, require training and practice, and have their figureheads and admirers.

Below: The pleasure of the powwow is readily apparent on the faces of these children at Lame Deer.

share with others and join in these celebrations of life. They continue to enrich us and expand our world view. Just like tribal members, the powwow and its people help me to learn and appreciate who I am, to cherish those things that make us alike and to respect those that make us different. Since I was born of a British father and an Italian mother in a country far from where I now reside, I am a mixture of cultures. I was raised to appreciate cross-culturalism. My upbringing has extended into my life as a "powwow person." My children are being brought up with the powwow as part of their world. They too are being raised to appreciate and enjoy differences in cultures. I know that they will be better individuals and lead richer lives because of their involvement as people of the circle. ✠

Above: Luke Whiteman, Blackfeet, wears primarily white on his right side and orange on his left. He uses tinsel tassels on his bustle tips. He and his brother, Stanley, are both champions who sometimes compete against each other in the adult Fancy division.

Facing page: Brooks Good Iron, a member of the Standing Rock Dakota tribe, makes his home in Fort Totten, North Dakota. An elder who wears the heavy full beadwork of a Traditional dancer, Brooks is highly respected for his dancing skill and his devotion to his native culture.

Above: *The setting sun lights up the face of this young Fancy dancer as it drops behind the mountains of Glacier National Park only twelve miles from Browning.*

Facing page: *Don Long Knife, Assiniboine, and his daughter, Erica, at Fort Belknap, Montana.*

Above: Mike Roberts, Choctaw/Chickasaw, calls Ada, Oklahoma, home, but travels north to Montana's North American Indian Days in summer for the cooler weather of the North Central Montana plains just east of the Rocky Mountains in Browning.

Left: The variations and similarities in Fancy regalia can be seen in this lineup of dancers after a contest at the Il-Wa-Sil Powwow in Seattle, Washington.

Above: Even at age five, Dakota Christian, Sioux, exudes the confidence and poise associated with being the accomplished Traditional dancer that he is.

Facing page: Poncho Brady, Arikara/Hidatsa, and Rebecca Hamilton, Sac-Fox/Kiowa/Apache, seem to have coordinated their dance clothes with each other and the rainbow overhead. Note the embroidery and complexity of Poncho's new Fancy dance clothes. Poncho dances very acrobatically and this new lighter outfit enables him to showcase the moves he develops in practice. Rebecca is well known on both the Northern and Southern circuits and serves as Head Lady dancer at many events.

BIBLIOGRAPHY AND VIDEOGRAPHY

△ △ △

Navajos have taken to the powwow within the past twenty years. These three dancers from Arizona came north to Arlee's annual powwow because of its reputation as a large and friendly event.

The following items marked with an asterisk are informative and entertaining. They are available from Meadowlark Communications, P.O. Box 7218, Missoula, MT 59807. Call the toll free phone number, 888-728-2180, for a current catalog.

BOOKS:

* DRUMBEAT...HEARTBEAT. Braine, Susan. Minneapolis, MN: Lerner Publications Company, 1995.

* EAGLE DRUM. Crum, Robert. New York, NY: Four Winds Press, Macmillan Publishing Company, 1994.

ETHNOMUSICOLOGY OF THE FLATHEAD INDIANS. Merriam, Alan P. Chicago, IL: Aldine, 1967.

* MONTANA'S INDIANS: YESTERDAY AND TODAY (SECOND EDITION). Bryan, William L. Jr.; photographs by Michael Crummett. Helena, MT: American and World Geographic Publishing, 1996.

NATIVE AMERICAN DANCE, CEREMONIES AND SOCIAL TRADITIONS. Heth, Charlotte, ed. Washington, DC: National Museum of the American Indian, Smithsonian Institution with Starwood Publishing, Inc., 1992.

* POWWOW. Ancona, George. New York, NY: Harcourt Brace and Company, 1992.

POWWOW. Horse Capture, George P. Cody, WY: Buffalo Bill Historical Center, 1989.

* POWWOW CALENDAR. Campbell, Liz. Summertown, TN: The Book Publishing Company, annual series.

* POWWOW COUNTRY. Roberts, Chris. Helena, MT: American and World Geographic Publishing, 1992.

* POWWOW: IMAGES ALONG THE RED ROAD. Marra, Ben. New York, NY: Abrams, 1996.

* POWWOW SUMMER. Rendon, Marcie R. Minneapolis, MN: Carolrhoda Books, The Lerner Group, 1996.

SONGS AND DANCES OF THE LAKOTA. Theisz, R.D. and Ben Black Bear, Sr. Rosebud, SD: Sinte Gleska College, 1976.

THROUGH THE EYE OF THE FEATHER. Tuchman, Gail. Layton, UT: Gibbs Smith, Publisher, 1994.

WAR DANCE: PLAINS INDIAN MUSICAL PERFORMANCE. Powers, William K. Tucson: University of Arizona Press, 1990.

* WE DANCE BECAUSE WE CAN. Bernstein, Diane Morris. Marietta, GA: Longstreet Press, Inc., 1996

VIDEO:

* CROW FAIR '95. Hardin, MT: Cold Camp Productions, 1995.

* CROW FAIR '96. Hardin, MT: Cold Camp Productions, 1996.

* CROW FAIR '97. Hardin, MT: Cold Camp Productions, 1997.

* DANCES FOR THE NEW GENERATIONS. American Indian Dance Theatre. Great Performances, Public Broadcasting Service. Available from Meadowlark Communications.

* ELEGANT VISIONS. Bartlesville, OK: Bartlesville Indian Women's Club, 1993.

* FINDING THE CIRCLE. American Indian Dance Theatre. Great Performances, Public Broadcasting Service. Available from Meadowlark Communications.

* GATHERING OF NATIONS '95. Albuquerque, NM: KASA-TV, 1995.

* GATHERING OF NATIONS '96. Albuquerque, NM: KASA-TV, 1996.

* GATHERING OF NATIONS '97. Albuquerque, NM: KASA-TV, 1997.

* HOW TO BEAD NATIVE AMERICAN STYLE, VOL. I, LOOM BEADWORK. Tulsa, OK: Full Circle Communications, 1994.

* HOW TO BEAD NATIVE AMERICAN STYLE, VOLUME 2, LAZY STITCH BEADWORK. Tulsa, OK: Full Circle Communications, 1995.

* HOW TO BEAD NATIVE AMERICAN STYLE, VOLUME 3, PEYOTE STITCH BEADWORK. Tulsa, OK: Full Circle Communications, 1996.

* HOW TO BEAD NATIVE AMERICAN STYLE, VOLUME 5, TWO NEEDLE APPLIQUÉ STITCH BEADWORK. Tulsa, OK: Full Circle Communications, 1996.

* HOW TO DANCE NATIVE AMERICAN STYLE. Tulsa, OK: Full Circle Communications, 1996.

* INTO THE CIRCLE. Tulsa, OK: Full Circle Communications, 1992.

* NATIVE AMERICAN MEN'S AND WOMEN'S DANCE STYLES #1. Tulsa, OK: Full Circle Communications, 1996.

* NATIVE AMERICAN MEN'S AND WOMEN'S DANCE STYLES #2. Tulsa, OK: Full Circle Communications, 1996.

* ON THE POWWOW TRAIL. Denver, CO: King of the Mountain Productions, 1993.

* POWWOW TIME, VOLUME 1: WELL AND ALIVE. Window Rock, AZ: Cool Runnings Production, 1996.

* POWWOW, A WARRIOR'S DREAM. Portage La Prairie, Manitoba, Canada: Wind Storm Productions, presented by Dakota Tipi First Nation, 1996.

* POWWOW CANADIAN STYLE. Saskatoon, Saskatchewan, Canada: Turtle Island Music, 1997.

* WACIPI POWWOW. St. Paul, MN: Twin Cities Public Television, 1995.

* WISCONSIN POWWOW AND NAAMIKAAGED: DANCER FOR THE PEOPLE, 2-volume set: Washington, DC: Smithsonian Folkways, 1996.

MAGAZINES AND NEWSPAPERS:

The following magazines and newspapers are excellent sources of information about Native American culture. Powwows are frequently featured.

Parfit, Michael. "Powwow" NATIONAL GEOGRAPHIC, June 1994.

ABORIGINAL VOICES; 201-116 Spadina Ave., Toronto, ON M5V 2K6, Canada. 800-324-6067

COWBOYS AND INDIANS; 128 Grant Ave., Santa Fe, NM 87501. 505-989-3400

INDIAN ARTIST; P.O. Box 5465, Santa Fe, NM 87502-5465. 505-982-1600.

NATIVE PEOPLES; 5333 N. 7th, Suite C224, Phoenix, AZ 85014. 602-252-2236.

WHISPERING WINDS; P.O. Box 1390, Folsom, LA 70437-1390. 800-301-8009.

ALBERTA SWEETGRASS; 15001 112th Ave., Edmonton, AB Canada T5M 2V6. 403-455-2945

INDIAN COUNTRY TODAY; 1920 Lombardy Dr., Rapid City, SD 57701. 605-341-0011.

NEWS FROM INDIAN COUNTRY; Rte 2 Box 2900-A, Hayward, WI 54843. 715-634-5226.

THE INDIAN TRADER; Box 1420, Gallup, NM 87305. 800-748-1624.

WHITE BUFFALO GAZETTE; 7530 South Broadway, Wichita, KS 67233. 316-524-1210.

WINDSPEAKER; 15001 112th Ave., Edmonton, AB Canada T5M 2V6 403-455-2700.

BIBLIOGRAPHY AND VIDEOGRAPHY

Sometimes a first person's name is all that is needed to identify him. Especially when that name is a part of his regalia. In this case the name belongs to champion Fancy dancer Spike Draper who was taking a break at Fort Belknap.

Chris Roberts and his son Corey at the Schemitzun Powwow in Hartford, Connecticut.

Since the publication of his first book *Powwow Country*, in 1992, Roberts has devoted his energies full-time to photography and writing.

Roberts' photographs have appeared in numerous books and magazine articles, are available as notecards and a series of trading cards and appear in the 1998 Powwow wall calendar. Currently Roberts is completing the photography for a 1999 Powwow calendar, and is developing a novel combining his past experiences in the music business with the powwow world.

A resident of Missoula, Montana, Chris has been dancing on the powwow circuit for thirty years. Originally from England, he had his first contact with Indian culture as a small boy. He is dedicated to depicting the richness of American Indian cultures, and the warm spirit of North America's native peoples.